W9-DDI-282

The Time Chunking Method

A 10-Step Action Plan For Increasing Your Productivity

An ArtOfProductivity.com Action Guide

Damon Zahariades

Copyright © 2017 by Damon Zahariades

All rights reserved. No part of this publication may be reproduced, distributed, or transmitted in any form or by any means, including photocopying, recording, or other electronic or mechanical methods, without the prior written permission of the publisher, except in the case of brief quotations embodied in critical reviews and certain other noncommercial uses permitted by copyright law. For permission requests, contact the author through the website below.

Art Of Productivity
http://www.artofproductivity.com

Other Books by Damon Zahariades

Morning Makeover: How To Boost Your Productivity, Explode Your Energy, and Create An Extraordinary Life - One Morning At A Time!

Would you like to start each day on the right foot? Here's how to create quality morning routines that set you up for more daily success!

* * *

Fast Focus: A Quick-Start Guide To Mastering Your Attention, Ignoring Distractions, And Getting More Done In Less Time!

Are you constantly distracted? Does your mind wander after just a few minutes? Learn how to develop laser-sharp focus!

* * *

Small Habits Revolution: 10 Steps To Transforming Your Life Through The Power Of Mini Habits!

Got 5 minutes a day? Use this simple, effective plan for creating any new habit you desire!

* * *

To-Do List Formula: A Stress-Free Guide To Creating To-Do Lists That Work!

Finally! A step-by-step system for creating to-do lists that'll actually help you to get things done!

* * *

The 30-Day Productivity Plan: Break The 30 Bad Habits That Are Sabotaging Your Time Management - One Day At A Time!

Need a daily action plan to boost your productivity? This 30-day guide is the solution to your time management woes!

* * *

Digital Detox: Unplug To Reclaim Your Life

Addicted to technology? Here's how to disconnect and enjoy real, meaningful connections that lead to long-term happiness.

* * *

The Time Chunking Method: A 10-Step Action Plan For Increasing Your Productivity

It's one of the most popular time management strategies used today. Double your productivity with this easy 10-step system.

* * *

For a complete list, please visit
http://artofproductivity.com/my-books/

What You'll Find In The Time Chunking Method: A 10-Step Action Plan For Increasing Your Productivity

You've probably read about the productivity method outlined in this action guide. It's called time chunking. You may already be using it to streamline your workflow and increase your productivity. If so, good for you!

This guide starts by explaining the basics of how to use the technique. It then dives into how you can tweak it to fit your circumstances. I'll show you how to squeeze maximum mileage from it by making small adjustments to suit your workflow.

This guide is designed to spur you to take action. It's not a book to be read and filed away, never to be implemented to benefit your life. It's meant to *applied*. That's the only way it can help you to boost your daily productivity.

Your Free Gift

Before we get started, I'd like to offer you a free gift. It's my way of saying thanks for spending time with me in this book.

Your gift is a Special Report titled, "*Catapult Your Productivity! The Top 10 Habits You Must Develop To Get More Things Done.*" As the title suggests, it's a collection of 10 habits that will help you pave the way toward getting more done in less time.

Claim your copy of *Catapult Your Productivity* at the link below and join my mailing list:

http://artofproductivity.com/free-gift/

I'm willing to bet you'll find at least a few ideas covered in that Report that will surprise you.

How can you obtain a copy of *Catapult Your Productivity! The Top 10 Habits You Must Develop To Get More Things Done?* It's simple. Visit ArtOfProductivity.com and sign up for my email list (or simply click the link above). You'll receive immediate access to the Report in PDF format. You can read it online, download it or print it out. It's your choice.

Being on my email list also means you'll be the first to know when I release a new productivity book. I plan to release them at a steep discount (or even free) for the first 24 hours. By signing up for my list, you'll get early notification.

If you don't want to join my list, that's completely fine. It just means I need to earn your trust. With that in mind, I think you're going to love the information I've included in this action guide. Specifically, I think you're going to love what it can do in your life.

Without further ado, let's jump in.

Contents

Introduction: How I Stumbled Onto The Time Chunking Method

I used to be terrible at managing my time. Every day was filled with interruptions. When I was a cubicle jockey in Corporate America, people would drop by and share the latest news about their families, love interests or sexual escapades. I didn't invite them, but my inability to banish them probably served the same result.

When I left the corporate world behind to run my own business, things didn't get any better. People would call, knowing I was jobless and at home. They probably thought I was spending my days sitting in my bathrobe and watching reruns of the X-Files.

If you run your own business, I'm sure you can relate.

And what about those rare occasions when I managed to reserve extended blocks of time for myself? Times during which I should have been working? Well, I'd get distracted from the task at hand. Watching Chris Rock videos on YouTube seemed more interesting than building websites. Visiting my favorite forums and blogs seemed a lot more exciting than writing articles about automotive parts (or whatever was on my plate at the moment).

I was a mess. With a solid 16 hours at my disposal each day, I couldn't seem to get more than a few hours of work accomplished.

That's a big problem when you're running a business. If you don't do the work, you don't bring in the bucks. It's the simplest equation there is.

So, I started to research time management tips. I dove into it like a starving hyena attacks a side of beef.

That's when I stumbled upon the time chunking method. It was a breath of fresh air. In fact, it's not an exaggeration to say that it changed the way I work. It gave my day structure and showed me how to work efficiently. That in turn gave me the opportunity to spend more time on people and projects that were important to me.

I'm not going to lie. Using time chunks isn't magic. Like creating any habit, integrating it into your daily process is going to take time, effort and diligence. If you're like me, you'll experience more than a few false starts on the way to learning how to master your time.

Failure is fine as long as you learn from it. You need to identify and fix the problems that caused it. You and I will be talking about such problems in Step 4 in this action guide.

We have a lot to cover in the pages that follow. We're going to move quickly so you can start using the information as soon as possible. None of it will do you any good unless you apply it to your daily process.

True learning comes with *application*.

Whenever you create a new habit (or break an unhealthy one), it's important to know why you're doing it. So we're going to start off by noting how the time chunking method can improve your life.

If you've never used this approach to getting things done,

you're in for a treat. It's a great strategy for managing your workflow. If you *have* used it, but never fully invested yourself in it, don't worry. We're going to cover ideas and systems that will help you to fully harness its value in your work.

Enough specious claptrap. Let's get this party started.

Step 1

List The Ways Using The
Time Chunking Method Will
Improve Your Life

List The Ways Using The Time Chunking Method Will Improve Your Life

Knowing the reasons you want to use the time chunking method is the key to making it a habit in your daily process.

* * *

Reasons drive action. You need to have a reason for doing something in order to make performing that task worth your time and effort. Moreover, your reason needs to be compelling enough to spur you onward when you hit roadblocks.

For example, suppose you want to start exercising on a regular basis. If you don't have a reason to do so, you're almost guaranteed to stop at some point (I speak from experience). But just having a reason isn't good enough. It needs to be compelling.

Let's say you've decided to exercise because you saw the movie *Fight Club* and would like a physique that looks like Brad Pitt's. Or if you're a lady, maybe you're dying to look like Jillian Michaels. Either way, that's not going to spur you onward when you're tired, under the weather and just plain lazy.

It's not a sufficiently compelling reason.

But suppose you've suffered a heart attack. Your doctor

visits your hospital bed and tells you the episode occurred because you're overweight and your coronary arteries are clogged. He advises you to trim down and cut out the junk food. If you don't, you could suffer another heart attack. Worse, you may not survive.

That's a compelling reason to make a change. The stakes are high. If you miss a day of exercise, or you surrender to your craving for pizza, it will (hopefully) motivate you to get back on track.

Now, with that in mind, let's consider why you'd want to adopt the time chunking technique.

It's not enough to just want to be more productive. That goal *sounds* good, but doesn't actually convey anything of value. It's something people say because no one wants to be *less* productive. In other words, that "goal" is not sufficiently compelling. It doesn't offer the proper motivation. It won't spur you onward when you confront obstacles (and believe me, you *will* confront them).

Drill down further. Ask yourself how your life would improve if you were able to work more productively? To get your creative juices flowing, here are some of my own goals:

- experience less stress throughout the day (or week)
- sleep more effectively due to less stress
- work fewer hours per day without suffering a decline in income
- work the same number of hour per day and enjoy an income boost
- have more time to spend with my loved ones

- accomplish production-related goals more quickly
- create and ship more products

Some of your goals are going to mirror my own. That's understandable. Everyone wants to experience less stress, sleep better, and make more money. But some of your goals are going to be uniquely yours.

For example, you might want to improve your reputation among your peers. Or working more efficiently may give you a boost of self-confidence. You might want more time to play coffee house gigs with your Stevie Ray Vaughan tribute band. Maybe you want to have more time at your disposal to care for your ailing parents.

The more specific your goals, the more compelling they're likely to be. The details are going to be critical as you train yourself to use time chunks in your daily workflow.

Don't skip this step. It's arguably the most important one of the bunch.

A quick word of caution: you'll be tempted to just think about the ways in which the time chunking method will improve your life, and leave it at that. I highly recommend creating a list you can regularly refer to. Write down your reasons for taking action on a piece of paper and tape that paper to the wall of your office. Or create your list in Google Docs. Then, print a copy to post on your wall.

There's something powerful about having your goals written in front of you. It prompts action. It spurs you to achieve them.

Once you've completed this first essential step, it's time to learn the basics of the time chunking approach. Onward to Step 2.

Step 2

Familiarize Yourself With The
Mechanics Of The Time
Chunking Method

Familiarize Yourself With The Mechanics Of The Time Chunking Method

As Beethoven was rumored to have said, you need to learn the rules before you can break them.

* * *

In this step, we're going to cover how the time chunking method works. These are the basics. You can find them detailed on virtually every website that discusses the technique.

I toyed with the idea of skipping this step. You probably know the information that follows. But ultimately, failing to describe the fundamentals of the technique in a quick-start action guide like the one you're reading seemed wrong. So, let's take a look at how time chunking was originally designed to be used.

Fair warning: we're going to move quickly through this step. That way, we can get to the meat of this guide - how to use time chunks in your daily workflow and adjust them to fully complement your life.

How Time Chunking Works
In A Nutshell

You're supposed to schedule your workday in 30-minute chunks. The first 25 minutes of each chunk is spent doing a particular task or batch of tasks (we'll talk about batching in a moment). After 25 minutes of work, you take a 5-minute break.

You're not supposed to maintain that pace for the entire day. If you try to do so, you'll burn out. At the end of the work segment of your 4th chunk, treat yourself to a 15-minute break.

Here's how that schedule appears on paper:

- Work for 25 minutes
  - Take a 5-minute break
- Work for 25 minutes
  - Take a 5-minute break
- Work for 25 minutes
  - Take a 5-minute break
- Work for 25 minutes
  - Take a **15-minute** break

You can do whatever you'd like during your breaks as long as it fits into 5 minutes. Five minutes may not seem like a lot of time, but that's the point. You're not giving yourself an opportunity to watch the latest episode of *The Walking Dead*.

You're giving yourself just enough time to stretch your legs or grab a quick snack.

Then, it's time to jump into another 25-minute work segment.

In Chapter 8, I'll give you a laundry list of things you can do on your breaks. That list is composed mainly of things I like to do. But I've included a lot of other ideas you'll love too.

But that's for later. Let's get back on track.

Working On Single Activities Vs. Working In Batches

Focus on performing a single task during your 25-minute work segments. If you're writing a blog post, ignore everything that's unrelated to writing that post until the 25 minutes of your current segment elapses. If you're working on a Profit & Loss report for your business, concentrate on getting that report done.

That means ignoring distractions. (I know, it's easier said than done.) In Chapter 4, I'll give you a few tips for minimizing the effect distractions have on your day as you incorporate the time chunking method into your life.

There will be times when you'll have a lot of small, related items on your ever-growing to-do list. Examples include paying your car insurance, emptying the kitchen trash, and throwing your laundry into the washer. None of those items will take 25 minutes. You'll probably be able to complete most of them in 2 or 3 minutes.

In those cases, working in batches can be an extremely effective in tactic for managing your time. Batch related tasks together and devote an entire 25-minute work segment to completing them. Doing so reduces distraction during that period. The less distracted you are, the more productive you'll be.

Batch processing works. It's an effective way to get a lot done without getting lost in a huge pool of tiny tasks. As a bonus, you'll get to cross a lot of to-do items off your list. That alone is worth giving it a try.

One quick note: batch processing has nothing to do with multi-tasking. When you batch your work, you're still concentrating on a single task at a time. You're just going through a laundry list of tasks, one by one, during the same 25-minute work segment.

What To Do When You Finish A Task Before 25 Minutes Elapses

You're not going to finish every task in 25 minutes. Some are going to take longer. Some are going to take a lot longer. You may find yourself devoting several time chunks to completing them.

You'll inevitably find yourself finishing tasks in the middle of your time chunks - for example, after 10 minutes of work. What should you do with the extra time?

Technically, you're supposed to use whatever time remains in the chunk to review your work or improve it in some way. But suppose you've taken a task as far as you can - or desire to - take it. What should you do then?

Simply abort the current time chunk. End it and take a 5-minute break. Then, review your to-do list, pick another task and start a new time chunk.

Why The Time Chunking Method Is So Effective

There are 4 reasons time chunking helps people to become more productive:

1. it limits the amount of time the brain has to focus.
2. it demolishes the tendency to procrastinate.
3. it reduces distraction borne of multitasking.
4. it pushes the individual toward *completing* tasks rather than just working on them.

The brain can only focus on a particular task for short periods of time. The time chunking approach works within the constraints of that limitation. It shortens the length of time the brain has available to focus to 25 minutes.

Regarding reason #2, all of us procrastinate. Show me someone who claims not to do so and I'll show you someone who is either delusional or disingenuous. The tendency to procrastinate is rooted in a lack of motivation. That problem affects every living person.

The time chunking system is designed to override that lack of motivation by breaking down the workday into easy-to-manage 30-minute chunks. Anyone can work for 25 minutes, followed by a 5-minute break, regardless of whether he or she is motivated to do so.

You already know that distractions kill your productivity. What many people don't realize is that multitasking opens the door to distraction and practically begs it to come inside. Using short time chunks eliminates the natural inclination to multitask, and thereby decreases our susceptibility to distraction.

Finally, the time chunking technique is designed to encourage the act of *completing* tasks. That's critical if you constantly find yourself spending more time than necessary on tasks. When you work in 25-minute segments, you become keenly aware of how long a particular task is taking you to finish. That's a huge motivator for getting it done.

A Few Last Words On The Mechanics Of Using Time Chunks

The time chunking method, as it was originally designed to be used, may seem rigid. You might even consider it draconian. But keep in mind that the basics I've outlined in Step 2 are exactly that: basics. Nothing more. They can - and should - be adjusted to complement your daily process.

That's what this action guide is about: making the time chunking approach work for you given your circumstances, not arbitrarily sticking to a strict system that may not suit you.

With that in mind, let's forge onward to Step 3…

Step 3:

Adjust The Time Chunking Method
To Suit Your Lifestyle

Adjust The Time Chunking Method
To Suit Your Lifestyle

Any habit you adopt, including the use of time chunks,
is only as useful as the extent to which it improves your
life.

* * *

You've probably heard a lot of people regaling the benefits of using
the GTD (Get Things Done®) system. Others follow the simpler
"7 Habits Of Highly Effective People®" system by the late Stephen
Covey. (Technically, Covey's "Habits" model is designed to be a
goal attainment system rather than a productivity system. But that
doesn't stop folks from using it as the latter.) Still others use
something called the Eisenhower Matrix.

But there's an important point missing in the discussion,
whether that discussion revolves around GTD, Covey's
"Habits," or any other productivity system...

Personal suitability.

In order for any system to work in your life, it needs to
complement your work process. The time chunking method is
supposed to improve your work process so you can get more
done in less time. Notice that you're not *discarding* your current
way of getting work done. Rather, you're breaking it down to
its core parts, removing the chaff and building good habits on
top of what remains.

That means the time chunking system, or any productivity system for that matter, must accommodate the basic principles that define how you work. If it doesn't, it's doomed to fail.

I'll use a personal example to illustrate this point…

How To Fail At Being More Productive: A Personal Example

I've been interested in boosting my productivity for more years than I can count. Even when I wasn't willing to put in the work to manage my time more effectively - and mind you, doing so *does* require work - I was always reading about it. That was my passive-aggressive way of trying to become more productive.

Needless to say, it didn't work.

When I finally got my proverbial rear in gear and dedicated myself to managing my time effectively, I tried several systems. I ultimately abandoned each of them for one reason or another. They gelled poorly with my workflow, used silly organizational tools or were just too complicated.

I eventually stumbled onto David Allen's Getting Things Done® system. It was new and sexy, and everyone was talking about it. Some folks went so far as to say that GTD was the only time management solution worth considering.

I decided to give it a try.

Now, let's put things on pause for a moment and talk about GTD. If you know anything about it, you know it encourages you to write down every single task on a list (or multiple lists that are each defined by when you need to get things done). If you have a large task that is composed of lots of smaller tasks, you're supposed to break the large task down. Every small task then gets put on one the lists.

The idea is to get everything out of your head so you can focus on the job at hand.

As you complete each task on your list, you cross it off. There's a lot more to GTD, such as implementing a tracking and retrieval system for your various to-do tasks. But I'm trying to keep things simple for the purpose of my example.

Here's the punchline: GTD was a major fail for me. Or maybe I failed GTD. Either way, it didn't work for me. Here's why:

I was overwhelmed by my task lists. Over the course of several days, I wrote down everything I needed to get done today, the next day, the following week and next month. I added things I wanted to accomplish by next year, in 3 years and even further down the road.

By the end of the 5th day, there were hundreds of items on my lists. Worse, I added new tasks each day. My lists never shrunk. On the contrary, they formed a collective mountain of to-do items that sucked the motivation out of me.

And when I accomplished something that I knew was on one of my lists, I had trouble finding the darn thing so I could cross it off!

I'll admit that I may have implemented the system poorly. GTD is complicated, and I'm a simple guy. That's not a great combo. Ultimately, when the dust cleared, it was obvious that GTD was a less-than-ideal time management system for me.

And that brings us back to the time chunking method...

How To Modify The Time Chunking Method To Complement Your Workflow

Recall the basics of using time chunks. You work for 25 minutes, then take a 5-minute break. After your 4th time chunk - or technically, the work segment of your 4th time chunk - you take a 15-minute break.

Let me be honest: that schedule doesn't work for me. It doesn't suit my workflow.

I write a lot. I write for clients, I write books, I write a blog, and I write for myself. When I write, I like to find a groove. When I'm in a groove, I can write like the wind, composing beautiful prose quickly.

Here's the problem: any type of interruption disrupts my flow. When that flow dies, so does my momentum. It takes me at least 20 minutes to find it again. Sometimes, I never find it.

I used to set my timer for 25 minutes. It would go off and completely disrupt my writing groove. I'd spend my 5-minute break worrying about whether I'd find it again. When I sat down at my computer for the next 25-minute work session, writing was a struggle.

So I modified the time chunking method to suit my workflow. Today, I use the following schedule:

- Work for 50 minutes
  - Take a 10-minute break
- Work for 50 minutes
  - Take a 10-minute break
- Work for 50 minutes
  - Take a 40-minute break
- Work for 50 minutes
  - Take a 10-minute break
- Work for 50 minutes
  - Take a 20-minute break
- Work for 50 minutes
  - Call it a night!

You'll notice the duration of the work segments is longer (50 minutes vs. 25 minutes). You'll also notice the duration of my breaks is longer (10 minutes vs. 5 minutes). Also, rather than sticking to the traditional 4-chunk cycle, I follow a 3-chunk cycle.

Fifty minutes gives me a lot more time to write once I've found a groove. That's important to me. When my timer finally goes off, it's a welcome disruption because I need a break.

Personally, I don't need a break every 25 minutes. Taking one that often actually impairs my productivity. I've trained myself to focus for 50 minutes and enjoy the longer 10-minute break that follows the work segment. During the 40-minute break at the end of my 3-chunk cycle, I grab a meal or take a nap depending on the time of day.

Ignore the purists. Feel free to alter the time chunking method in whatever way will best suit your lifestyle and workflow. For example, modify the length of your work segments and breaks to give yourself time to find a groove. Adjust them to create a daily schedule that allows you to maximize the amount of time you spend with your family.

If you're in a groove and making a lot of progress when your timer goes off, don't feel like you have to stop everything and take a break. Keep working if doing so will help you finish the task at hand more quickly.

Just keep in mind that the brain can only focus for short periods of time. Once you reach the end of that period, there's a steep decline in productivity. It will look something like the following...

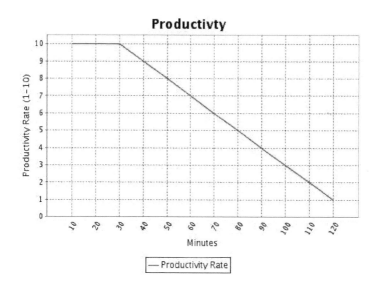

Productivty

Last Words On Modifying The Time Chunking Method

Don't look at the time chunking method as a pair of handcuffs. No one is forcing you to adhere to a strict set of rules. Instead, test how you perform over different periods of time. Try 25-minute segments for a week and monitor your performance. Test 40-minute segments the following week. Then, try 60-minute segments.

Experiment with different break periods. Five minutes doesn't work for me, especially after a 50-minute work segment. But it may work perfectly for you. The only way you'll know for certain is to conduct tests and track your results. Try 7 minutes, 10 minutes, or even 15 minutes. Note how efficiently you're able to work.

If you have superhuman focus in the morning, but the focus of a bored 3-year-old in the afternoon, test the following schedule:

- Work for 90 minutes
  - Take a 15-minute break
- Work for 60 minutes
  - Take a 10-minute break
- Work for 50 minutes
  - Take a 10-minute break
- Work for 40 minutes

- Take a 10-minute break
- Work for 30 minutes
  - Take a 15-minute break

Remember, you're in control. Design any schedule that might suit you. Then, try it out and track how it impacts your workflow and output.

Now, let's talk about some of the hurdles you'll confront on the way to becoming a time chunking master.

Step 4

Plan For The Challenges You'll Face While Creating The Time Chunking Habit

Plan For The Challenges You'll Face While Creating The Time Chunking Habit

Every attempt to establish a new habit is beset by obstacles. Train yourself to conquer them.

* * *

Nothing comes easy. You'll discover that as you implement the time chunking method into your daily work process. Building good habits (and breaking bad ones) is tough. The brain gets into a rhythm and resists change.

In this step, we'll take a close look at the various obstacles you'll face as you practice using time chunks. Be warned: they come in many forms and some are less than obvious. But left unchecked, all of them can become major problems in your pursuit of increased productivity.

Along the way, I'll make several suggestions that will help you to deal with these challenges. Most of them will be intuitive. That's fine as long as they work. The key is setting the habit and reinforcing it with consistent, repeated action.

With that out of the way, let's discuss a problem that every person alive can relate to…

Interruptions From Co-Workers, Friends, And Family Members

When you have a full-time job, coworkers can become a major problem. They drop by your office or cubicle without warning and ask (disingenuously), "Hey, got a second?" When I worked in Corporate America, I always wanted to respond, "Sure. For you, I have 2 seconds. Make it fast." That would not have helped my career, so naturally I refrained from making such comments.

When you run your own business or work from home, friends and family members become the culprits. They don't mean to prevent you from getting things done. But they'll assume you'll surrender to their requests for attention because they don't think you have a "real job."

I'll give you an example from my own experience.

When I left my corporate job to start my own business, some of my friends and family had the impression that I was suddenly had a lot of free time on my hands. I certainly didn't give them that notion. But they had it nonetheless.

I'd get phone calls throughout the day from folks who "wanted to say hello." Occasionally, people would even stop by to "chat for a minute."

I normally look forward to connecting with the people in my life. Life is very bland without our loved ones. But if I'm writing an article or analyzing metrics for one of my websites, I need to focus. I need to find a groove. Interruptions destroy grooves.

If you hope to use the time chunking method to boost your output, you'll need to eliminate - or at least minimize - the number of interruptions that occur during the course of your day. Here are 5 suggestions for doing that:

1. turn off your phone
2. close your email client
3. discourage co-workers from dropping by without an appointment
4. tell friends and family members that you'll return calls at the end of the day
5. if someone drops by your home, do not answer the door

Turning off your phone and closing your email client are easy. Getting co-workers, friends and family members to respect your time is more difficult. You need to set expectations. You need to train them to respect your time.

It worked for me. It'll work for you too. Just be ready to receive a few uncomfortable glares when you outline the new expectations to the people in your life.

Lack Of Motivation To Maintain A High Level Of Productivity

Staying productive for an hour is easy. Anyone can do it. Staying productive throughout the day is far more difficult, even while using the time chunking method. It requires focus and discipline.

And staying productive day after day, when you're tired and would rather be doing 100 other things than work? That's even harder. The only way to do it is by creating a habit and reinforcing it with daily action.

Why is it so hard to stay productive while using the time chunking method? It boils down to a simple problem: a lack of motivation. If you find yourself becoming lax in your use of time chunks, it's because you're not properly motivated to use them.

Recall Step 1, where you came up with reasons to work more efficiently. Those reasons - e.g. to spend more time with your family, generate more income, get more sleep, etc. - are your motivation. If laziness is preventing you from using time chunks, that's a sign that your reasons are not sufficiently compelling to you.

Imagine that your next meal was dependent on whether you stuck to your time chunks. If you miss one, you don't eat. That's a compelling reason to stay on track. It's *motivating*.

So if you're having trouble making the time chunking

method stick in your daily workflow, revisit your reasons for creating the habit. You may need to tweak them to make them more compelling. Or you might only need a reminder about why you're working so hard.

Distractions From The Task At Hand

Distractions are everywhere. From social media and your favorite blogs to the refrigerator, television and video games, you're constantly being enticed to abandon the work in front of you. Worse, if you surrender to the temptation, it's easy to lose track of time.

For example, you tell yourself that you're only going to check CNN.com for new headlines, but end up spending 20 minutes reading the articles. Or you convince yourself that you're only going to check your favorite online forum for new threads, but become embroiled in an argument about politics with other members. Whoosh! Forty-five minutes gone.

I speak from experience.

Distractions are incredibly damaging to your productivity. They're insidious and seductive. They promise immediate gratification, but suck you into activities that can last hours if you lack the discipline to pull yourself away from them.

That's the reason every productivity expert recommends learning to ignore distractions. The problem is, that isn't very helpful. In fact, it's trite, useless advice.

The missing ingredient is how to actually do it.

I'm in the process of writing a book on how to keep distractions at bay. It's a large subject that deserves more time than can be devoted to it here. Having said that, here are a few tips that have worked for me:

- **Declutter your desk.** If there's an item on your desk that's unnecessary to get the current task completed, put it away. If you never use that item, throw it out.

- **Turn off your phone.** I mentioned this earlier, and it's important enough to repeat it. Seriously, turn off your phone.

- **Install a browser extension that blocks your access to certain sites.** There's no shortage of these tools. If you use Chrome, look for StayFocusd or Strict Workflow in the Chrome web store. (Strict Workflow is designed to complement the time chunking method.) If you're on a Mac, check out WasteNoTime and Mindful Browsing.

Nothing trumps discipline. Ideally, you should be able to work without having to use site-blocking browser extensions to keep you on track. Having said that, using such tools can be a great way to train yourself to ignore one of the worst distractions you'll face while working: the internet.

Ideas That Are Unrelated To The Task At Hand

This used to be a huge problem for me.

I'm continuously thinking of new ideas. Each one that springs to mind begs to be researched immediately. For example, in the middle of working on a blog post for a client, I'd suddenly come up with a multi-faceted content marketing plan for another client. Blog posts, landing pages, press releases, reports, lead magnets for an email list, etc.

And off I'd go to flesh out that plan and research its various components. Then, while working on it, I'd be struck with another completely unrelated idea for another client. Was I disciplined enough to focus on the idea I was already working on? Of course not. Off I'd go again.

That's hardly a productive way to work.

I'll bet you can relate to this problem. Maybe you're constantly coming up with ideas to grow your business. Or perhaps you're always thinking of tasks you need to complete. Dropping everything to research those ideas or perform those tasks will, of course, demolish your current time chunk.

So, I'm going to give you the cure. It's simplicity itself. Whenever you're struck by a new idea or errant thought, write it down. Then, keep working.

Writing it down removes it from your mind so you can free up space to focus on the task in front of you. It also removes the chore of having to remember that idea or thought. That's one of the core principles of the Getting Things Done (GTD) system.

It works.

Unanticipated Emergencies

There's nothing you can do to shield yourself from unanticipated emergencies. When they occur, the only thing you can do is react to the circumstances. Of all the challenges you'll face when implementing the time chunking method into your workflow, this is the one over which you have zero control.

I'm mentioning it because you will, on occasion, have to abandon your time chunks. For example, your adolescent son will suffer an injury that needs medical attention; your teenage daughter's car will break down on the freeway; your spouse will urgently need you to pick something up at the grocery store.

There's little you can do to avoid these types of situations. Just realize that they'll happen on occasion. When they do, they'll ruin your productivity.

Sometimes, you have to roll with the punches.

In the next step, we're going to talk about timeboxing and how it relates to your use of the time chunking method. Although they're commonly thought of in the same context, they're completely different methods for improving your productivity.

Ready to jump in? Let's do it…

Step 5

Distinguish Between Timeboxing
And The Time Chunking Method

Distinguish Between Timeboxing And The Time Chunking Method

Timeboxing and the time chunking method offer different methods for accomplishing similar goals.

* * *

Timeboxing was around long before time chunking became popular. It's a method for limiting the amount of time allocated to a particular task or project. At the end of a timebox, the individual evaluates his or her progress on the activity at hand, and asks a simple question: "Does the work I've completed satisfy the job requirements?"

If the answer is yes, no more work is performed on the task or project. If the answer is no, further time boxes are scheduled as needed.

Timeboxing was originally created as a way for teams to manage projects. The goal was to reduce the likelihood that a given project would extend past its scope. In doing so, timeboxing helps the individual or team to meet the project's deadline.

One of the benefits of using time boxes in this manner is that it prevents you from falling prey to Parkinson's Law. That law states that "*work expands so as to fill the time available for its completion.*" If you allot 4 hours for a particular activity, that activity is likely to require 4 hours to complete. If you allot 1 hour, you're likely to complete it in 1 hour.

With timeboxing, you establish a limited time frame during which you'll work on an activity. Committing to that time frame sets a deadline. It forces you to work toward the completion of the activity rather than simply spending time working on it. Importantly, it also discourages perfectionism.

How Is Timeboxing Different From The Time Chunking Method?

The time chunking method is a type of timeboxing strategy. As we discussed at the beginning of this guide, it encourages you to work for 25-minute segments and take 5-minute breaks between them. (Again, I strongly recommend testing different durations and creating a modified time chunking system that complements your natural workflow and ability to focus.)

The duration of a time box can technically vary from a few minutes to several months. It depends on the activity or project. The latter might involve hundreds of individual tasks.

The time chunking method is intended to keep you on task. As we covered in Step 2, it was created with the idea that the brain can only focus for short periods of time. After that time elapses, it needs a short break.

Timeboxing was designed to manage projects in such a way that time isn't wasted on them. Again, it discourages perfectionism.

With the time chunking method, you have the flexibility to cater to your perfectionist tendencies. You can devote as many time chunks as you desire to a task. There's no formal evaluation step that forces you to assess your progress and determine if you've met a project's requirements.

That's a huge difference from timeboxing. With timeboxing, you set a deadline - for example, 2 hours - for each activity. The deadline is flexible. If, when it arrives, you haven't met the activity's requirements, you estimate the amount of additional time you need to devote to it and create another time box. Even though the deadline is flexible, it pushes you toward completion. It quiets your inner perfectionist and helps you focus on "shipping."

It's a powerful tool for increasing your productivity. So that begs the question…

Which Should You Choose: Timeboxing Or The Time Chunking Method?

In a word, both.

Your productivity is influenced by two things:

1. your ability to focus on the task at hand
2. your ability to ship

The time chunking method addresses your ability to focus, but not your ability to ship (at least, not directly). Timeboxing addresses your ability to ship, but not your ability to focus (at least, not directly).

Why not use both techniques simultaneously to address both issues? Here's an example:

Suppose you're writing a long blog post. From your experience writing similar blogs in the past, you know you can complete the first draft in 2 hours. Start with timeboxing. Set aside 2 hours to complete the draft. Now, use the time chunking method to break that 2-hour chunk into several work segments.

If you're using a typical time chunking model, your schedule will look like the following:

- Work for 25 minutes
  - Take a 5-minute break

- Work for 25 minutes
  - Take a 5-minute break
- Work for 25 minutes
  - Take a 5-minute break
- Work for 25 minutes
  - Take a **15-minute** break
- Work for 20 minutes to complete the task

That equals 2 hours of work.

Personally, I'd used a modified model that caters to my own natural workflow. It would look like the following:

- Work for 50 minutes
  - Take a 10-minute break
- Work for 50 minutes
  - Take a 10-minute break
- Work for 20 minutes
  - Take a 20-minute break

The point is that the time chunking method can work seamlessly with timeboxing to increase your daily output. Each is flexible enough to accommodate the other.

Some people swear by timeboxing and claim they wouldn't be able to work in any other fashion. Others swear by the time chunking method and make similar claims about its effectiveness. But there's no reason to choose between them. Use them both.

This guide is obviously about using the time chunking method. For that reason, I'm not devoting a significant amount of time on other time management strategies. But it's worth mentioning timeboxing as an important complement to using time chunks.

I encourage you to try it. In addition to working within time chunks, set time boxes that limit the amount of time you spend on projects. You'll find that it will cure you of your perfectionism. That alone will be a major step toward boosting your productivity.

What To Expect In The Rest Of This Action Guide

In the second half of this guide, we're going to focus on how you can fully leverage the time chunking method in your daily work. Step 6 will cover a laundry list of things you can do to get more out of every one of your work segments.

In Step 7, we'll focus on a serious problem that affects nearly every person who tries to boost his or her productivity: burnout. I'll give you several tips for avoiding it.

A lot of folks who start using the time chunking method are at a loss regarding what to do during their breaks. Step 8 will give you a plethora of useful ideas. We'll have some fun in that section of the guide.

In Step 9, we'll take a look at the basic tools you'll need to make the time chunking method work for you. We'll also discuss a number of apps that are currently available that claim to maximize your use of time chunks. My perspective might surprise you.

Finally, Step 10 will show you how to squeeze maximum value out of the time chunking method.

We still have a lot to cover, so let's get to it!

Step 6

Make Choices That Maximize Your Use
Of The Time Chunking Method

Make Choices That Maximize Your Use Of The Time Chunking Method

Your success with the time chunking method will be heavily influenced by the decisions you make ahead of time.

* * *

It's not enough to decide to use the time chunking method, even if you have compelling reasons for doing so. Developing the habit takes dedication and resolve. You're going to feel exhausted on some days. You're going to feel sluggish and lethargic. And you're going to get frustrated - with yourself and others.

Exhaustion, lethargy and frustration will impair your ability to use the time chunking method. They'll make it more difficult to create and maintain the habit. They'll make it easier to become distracted, even if you have major deadlines looming over your head.

There's a simple way to keep those challenges at bay: give your mind and body the resources they need to perform well. That's a big part of what we're going to address in this step.

What follows will sound familiar to you. The idea of getting sufficient sleep, regular exercise and eating healthy to perform well is hardly insightful. Grok and his buddies were probably doing those same things before heading out to hunt for food in paleolithic times. And they didn't even have the internet to guide them.

I'm going to tell you what works for me. Note that I'm not recommending that you do what I do. When it comes to sleep, exercise and diet, you should follow your doctor's advice. If you're 70 years old, coping with diabetes, and have a number of food allergies, you're going to need to follow a different regimen than a 25-year-old athlete.

We're also going to cover how to plan goals and track your progress. The only way to know whether the time chunking method is making you more productive is to monitor your output. I'll show you how I do it in the second half of Step 6.

With that out of the way, let's talk about your sleep...

The Value Of Sleep

You already know sleep is important. That should be intuitive. You feel rundown after a string of sleepless nights. By contrast, you feel rejuvenated after getting 8 hours of restful slumber. A large body of research backs that up. Numerous studies show that people perform more efficiently, make fewer errors and cause fewer accidents when they get an adequate amount of sleep each night.

The problem is that many people readily sacrifice sleep, either for fun or the facade of increased productivity. For example, you've probably stayed up late to watch a television program, knowing that you were not going to be able to recoup the lost slumber time.

You're not alone. Most people have done the same things at some point in their lives. Some do it on a regular basis.

A lot of people forgo sleep because they think doing so makes them more productive. After all, they're working when they would otherwise be sleeping. How could they not be more productive?

In reality, that's a mirage. Working longer hours doesn't make you more productive. At a certain point, it makes you *less* productive. A sleep-deprived individual is more likely to make mistakes and perform shoddy work. Mistakes need to be corrected. Shoddy work needs to be redone. That takes time, which demolishes your productivity.

So how much sleep do you need? Everyone's different. Personally, I perform well after sleeping 6 hours a night with a 20-minute nap in the afternoon. Others need 8 hours of sleep a night or they feel they're unable to concentrate. I've also met people who claim to do well with 4 hours and no naps. But I have my doubts.

A friend of mine follows a polyphasic sleep schedule to boost his productivity. His schedule looks like the following:

- 3 hours at night
- 20-minute nap at 10:30 a.m.
- 20-minute nap at 2:30 a.m.
- 20-minute nap at 6:30 a.m.

He claims it works. I've never done it, so I can't speak to its effectiveness. I'll be testing it soon, however, for a new book I'm writing on how sleep impacts your productivity.

As a general rule, plan to get at least 7 hours of sleep each night. Try to sneak in a 20-minute nap during the afternoon. You might be surprised at how refreshed you'll feel after just 20 minutes of shuteye.

If you're employed full-time, napping can be tricky. Most employers frown on employees sleeping at their desks. When I worked in Corporate America, I'd use part of my lunch hour. I'd get into my car, drive to a semi-deserted parking lot, park under a tree and catch a few winks.

The great thing about short, 20-minute naps is that you can easily fit them into your schedule. All you need is a little privacy.

How Exercise Affects Your Productivity

You already know the many physical and health-related benefits of regular exercise. Working out keeps your weight under control, prevents heart disease and stroke, and even helps to keep diabetes at bay. It also improves your sleep and strengthens your heart and lungs.

You probably also know that regular exercise introduces cognitive benefits. It puts you in a better mood, reduces your stress levels, improves your memory and can even slow cognitive decline.

It shouldn't come as a surprise that regularly working out can significantly boost your productivity. Studies show that it can dramatically increase your energy, especially if you lead a sedentary lifestyle. Ever felt exhausted after sitting in front of your computer all day? Researchers claim that 15 minutes of physical activity - doing something as simple as walking - will rejuvenate you.

If you feel more energetic, you'll be more likely to focus during your time chunks. Your mind will be less prone to distractions that threaten to pull your attention away from the task at hand. The result? You'll get more done.

The most common reason people give for not working out is that they lack the necessary time. But that reason is usually untrue. The decision to not exercise rarely has anything to do with time. Rather, it's a matter of priorities.

I'll give you an example from my own life.

When I left Corporate America to run my own business, I wasted a lot of time. I played video games and spent hours at the local coffee shop. And I got together with friends who were either unemployed, on vacation or retired. Because of these "demands" on my time, I convinced myself that I didn't have enough time to exercise.

But that was just an excuse.

While I could argue that those activities were important to relieve stress, doing so would be disingenuous. The truth is, I wasted a ton of time that could have otherwise been spent improving my health.

So, if you're not following a regular workout routine, ask yourself this question: is it because you lack the time or because you haven't given it a high priority in your life? If you're spending hours each week watching television, going out with friends and "engaging" on social media, it's probably the latter.

And that's okay. The important thing is that you're honest with yourself. That way, if you truly value your productivity, you can make a conscious decision to improve it via regular exercise.

Here are a few suggestions in the event you're compelled to start a workout routine…

- **Consult your doctor.** Your doctor will evaluate your health and tolerance for physical activity. That will become increasingly important as you grow older. Also, see your doctor before starting a workout routine if you cope with arthritis, osteoporosis or other maladies.

- **Start slow.** Once you're convinced that you should exercise, it's tempting to jump in with both feet. Resist the temptation. Start with 15 minutes of mild exercise, such as a brisk walk. As your stamina and cardiovascular strength improve, increase the time you spend working out.

- **Perform different types of exercises.** Don't focus solely on cardio routines. Devote time to strength training and flexibility training.

- **Don't wait to join a gym.** It's too easy to postpone exercise until you have time to join. Don't delay. You can do plenty of routines at home or at a local park. You don't need a treadmill to take a walk.

- **Invest in exercise equipment for your home.** I'm not a huge fan of gyms. First, they tend to be expensive. Second, they require you to travel back and forth from the gym. That wastes time. It also discourages you from going. Third, gyms foster a social environment. It's too easy to waste time socializing when you should be concentrating on your workout.

I plan to write an in-depth action guide in the near future that focuses on how you can leverage diet and exercise to boost your productivity. That guide will give this topic the attention it deserves. For now, I encourage you to start protecting your health so you're able to concentrate and work efficiently during your time chunks.

Speaking of diet…

Diet And The Time Chunking Method

The foods and drinks you consume each day are going to heavily influence your productivity. Eat the right stuff and you'll find it easier to stick to your time chunks and focus on your work. Regularly eat junk food (or skip meals) and your ability to focus will quickly erode. (Again, I speak from experience. I *love* junk food.) Even if you manage to stick to your time chunks, you'll work slower and the quality of your output will suffer.

Before you go through your kitchen and pantry and start chucking the cookies, chips and candy, let's talk about how food affects your mind and body.

Let's start with your mind.

When you eat something, the glucose level in your bloodstream rises. That glucose is absorbed by the cells in your body and stored for later use. A considerable portion is transported to the brain. There, it aids brain function, influencing everything memory and clarity of thinking to learning capacity and the ability to focus.

Can you see how that might affect your productivity? You need glucose to work efficiently.

You can obtain glucose from junk food or healthy food. A donut or piece of pizza will deliver it to your bloodstream as surely as a roast beef sandwich. The difference is in how that glucose is released into your blood.

When you eat junk food, the glucose is released quickly. It also dissipates quickly. You've seen kids on a sugar high. They run around like maniacs for a short period, fueled by the glucose. Then, they crash, sometimes falling asleep. That's the effect of junk food. As an adult, you (hopefully) won't run around like a maniac, but you will find it difficult to concentrate when you crash.

When you eat healthy food, the glucose is released slowly into your blood. It gives your brain energy over a much longer period. The result? You'll be able to concentrate and complete your work more quickly.

Bottom line: eat healthy to stay alert and focused during your workday.

Thus far, we've covered how your diet affects your mind. Let's now take a look at how your diet affects your body.

Regularly eating junk food will cause you to gain body fat. Keep in mind, that doesn't necessarily mean you'll gain weight. Some people follow a diet composed mainly of junk food. They don't gain a ton of weight because they're eating very little substantive food. Instead of beef, eggs, and select vegetables, they fill themselves with Red Vines, Doritos and Ben & Jerry's ice cream.

You've probably heard the term "skinny fat." It describes a slender person who has a large percentage of body fat. Being slender doesn't mean you're immune to the health problems experienced by overweight individuals. Excess body fat can wreak havoc on your hormones, particularly if you're a woman. It can also impair the function of your liver and serve as a storage mechanism for various toxins.

Those problems will definitely erode your ability to work productively.

Most people who follow a poor diet are overweight. Some are clinically obese. Compared to their healthier counterparts, they're more susceptible to a variety of debilitating health complications.

For example, obese individuals are more likely to develop coronary artery disease. That puts them at an increased risk of heart attack and stroke. They're also more likely to develop high blood pressure and type 2 diabetes. Studies show that obesity can lead to memory impairment, cognitive dysfunction and respiratory problems.

Those are scary consequences of following a poor diet. They can severely undermine your attempts to improve your productivity. It's hard to focus, even during a short time chunk, when you're uncomfortable, unfocused and in pain.

Bottom line: eat healthy to stay fit. You'll feel better, have more energy and be better able to concentrate on your work.

Having said that, following a proper diet will only take you so far. Another critical piece of the productivity puzzle is your stress level…

Stress: The Nemesis Of Productivity

Stress is unavoidable. It's a normal part of your brain's response to a perceived threat. The more demands on your time and attention, the more stress you'll experience. The most important point to remember - at least, in the context of your productivity - is that your ability to keep stress under control will influence your ability to work efficiently.

Most of us can handle a considerable amount of stress. We can get our work done even if we're fighting with our spouses, angry with our kids or dealing with an unpleasant boss. The problem is, many people fail to implement controls that prevent such circumstances from occurring at the same time.

The result? They experience rising stress levels and declining productivity levels. Some people even suffer serious health problems stemming from persistent levels of extreme stress in their lives. That further impacts their productivity.

So if stress is unavoidable, how can we protect our brains from becoming overloaded with it?

The solution is to install controls that limit others' access to - and influence over - you.

Admittedly, that's easier said than done. After all, you can't stop people from making demands on your time, can you?

You absolutely *can*.

A lot of the stress you experience on a daily basis is caused by interruptions. Every time someone interrupts your workflow, you need 15 to 20 minutes to get back on track. That not only destroys your current time chunk, but you may silently chastise yourself for allowing it to happen. You might also feel hostility toward the person who interrupted you, especially if you're trying to meet a looming deadline.

Those things cause stress. Worse, they do so subtly so you may not even realize it's happening.

We talked about how you can limit, and even eliminate, interruptions in Step 4. There's no need to repeat that discussion here. Suffice to say, eliminating interruptions will cause you to feel less stressed out.

Consider other things that might be adding stress to your life. Here are a few examples…

- your boss is demanding that you rush a project.
- your spouse is angry with you because you forgot to fill up the cars with gas.
- your son was suspended from his school because he got into a fight with another child.
- you feel guilty because you don't call your parents often enough.

You can influence the impact each of these items has on your stress level. By doing so, you can influence the effect each has on your productivity.

For example, suppose your boss is demanding that you meet an unreasonable deadline. Simply letting him or her know about the other projects on your plate may be enough to compel him to give you more time. Your boss may be completely unaware of the other demands on your time.

A lot of employees are unwilling to admit their limitations to their bosses for fear they might disappoint them and thereby hurt their careers. But struggling to meet unrealistic deadlines is a surefire recipe for high stress levels. And that is guaranteed to hurt your long-term productivity (which, of course, can hurt your career).

Most minor stressors can be eliminated by communicating with the involved parties. Talking with your spouse can relieve his or her anger. Sitting down with your son and explaining why fighting is usually a poor solution to problems can prevent future suspensions. Creating a schedule to call your parents - for example, every Sunday at 10:00 a.m. - can alleviate feelings of guilt over lack of contact.

What about more significant events that are outside your control? Here are a few examples...

- your household budget is in ruins due to a costly medical emergency.
- your car is in the shop and needs a new transmission.
- your beloved dog suddenly dies after developing a health condition.
- your house is burglarized.

Such events will cause you to feel a considerable amount of stress. They can make it difficult to focus and complete your work.

Here, it's important that you take steps to control the stress. Otherwise, it will sap your energy, make you irritable, reduce your creativity and even lead to depression. Here are a few tips for keeping your brain in check when life throws a curve ball:

- **Keep a stress journal**. Write down how you feel and the circumstances in your life that are causing you to experience those feelings.
- **Set aside time for activities you enjoy**. That might include reading, gardening, going out to eat with your spouse, or playing board games with your kids.
- **Take a walk**. Walking is one of the most therapeutic activities you can enjoy when you're under extreme stress.
- **Talk to your spouse**. Sharing your thoughts with your spouse can make the stressor seem less of a crisis.

The takeaway is that high stress levels can severely hamper your ability to work productively. That being the case, it's important to take steps designed to keep them under control.

Let's now talk about goal-setting. Without clearly-defined goals, it's difficult to know whether the work you're doing during your time chunks is moving you in the right direction.

And if it's not moving you in the right direction, what's the point of doing it?

Set Daily, Weekly And Monthly Goals

The art of setting goals is usually oversimplified. Most people forge ahead without giving much thought to the type of goals they should set or the traits that characterize a proper goal.

Then, weeks or months down the road, they wonder why they failed to accomplish whatever they set out to do.

The reason for their failure can usually be traced back to the goal itself, as opposed to a personal deficit that's preventing them from accomplishing it. Their goal was improperly conceived and therefore lacked the proper support.

For example, a lot of people want to lose weight. That alone is not a well-conceived goal. It lacks specificity. It also lacks a way for the individual to track her progress (losing a ½ pound would technically meet her goal). Moreover, there's no way to know whether her reasons for wanting to lose weight are compelling enough to prompt her to take action. (We discussed the power of identifying compelling reasons in Step 1.)

Before you can set goals, you need to understand what constitutes a proper one. Here are 4 traits every goal you set for yourself should have:

1. Specificity
2. Tracking support
3. Complementary to your desired lifestyle
4. Realistic

Suppose you're a novelist. Your income is heavily influenced by your output. Therefore, you want to be prolific. You want to be more like Stephen King and less like J.D. Salinger.

Specificity means that your goal must be precise. An example might be to *"write 60,000 words in my current novel during April."*

Tracking support means having a way to track your progress. For example, April has 30 days. Therefore, you must write at least 2,000 a day to meet your goal.

Complementary to your desired lifestyle means that achieving your goal should move you closer to living the life you want to lead. Let's say you currently have a full-time job, but aspire to make a living from your novels. *"Write 60,000 words in my current novel during April"* complements your desired lifestyle.

Realistic means your goal should be achievable. Suppose you work full-time, care for your ailing parents, and volunteer at a local food bank during weekends. You probably won't be able to write 2,000 words a day. That goal would be unrealistic - or at least highly optimistic - given your current circumstances.

An Example Of How To Create Goals For Your Time Chunks

Now that you're familiar with the traits of a proper goal, set goals related to your use of the time chunking method.

Let's continue with our previous example. You're a novelist and want to write 60,000 words in your new novel during April. You're using a conventional 25/5 time chunk (work for 25 minutes, break for 5 minutes).

Simply sticking to that schedule won't tell you if you're on track to meeting your goal. At the end of the day, you may only have written 1,500 words despite sticking to a 25/5 time chunking regimen.

I'll show you how to solve that problem below.

The solution is to create a monthly goal and work backwards to create weekly and daily goals. For our example, we already have our monthly goal: to write 60,000 words during April. That translates into 15,000 words per week, which, in turn, means writing 2,143 words per day. Because April has 30 days, we'll round that figure to 2,000 words. (It simplifies the math.)

Let's say you're able to write 400 words during each time chunk. That means you need to complete 5 time chunks each day to stay on track toward meeting your goal.

Suppose you want to take Sundays off. Instead of 7 days, you'll only have 6 days each week to write 15,000 words. That means you'll need to write 2,500 words a day rather than 2,000

(15,000 divided by 6). At a rate of 400 words per time chunk, you'd need to complete 7 time chunks to stay on track.

Hopefully, you recognize the importance of setting goals with respect to maximizing your use of the time chunking method. Your goals allow you to monitor your progress, whether you're trying to complete a project that's due tomorrow or one due next month (or even next year). They're essential to your ability to work productively.

Before we close out this step, let's talk briefly about the basic mechanics of tracking your progress.

How To Track Your Progress While Using Time Chunks

The manner in which you track your progress will be influenced by the type of work you do. If you're a novelist, you'll want to track your daily, weekly and monthly word count. If you're a college student, you may want to track your study time. If you're a stay-at-home parent, tracking may entail noting the activities you perform and tasks you complete during your time chunks each day.

The purpose of tracking your progress is that it gives you an opportunity to evaluate your past performance. That, in turn, may reveal aspects of your workflow that can be improved.

My favorite tracking tool is Google Sheets. It's not only free, but it's in the cloud. That means I can access and update my sheets whether I'm at home on my PC, at the coffee shop on my Chromebook or at a friend's house on his Mac.

You might be surprised by the simplicity of my spreadsheets. Writing is a large part of my business, so I track my daily word count. Here are the items I include in my sheets:

- date
- day of the week
- word count for the day (I also have a running total at the bottom of my sheet).
- average word count for each time chunk (this gets a bit

murky since I vary the length of my time chunks)
- number of time chunks completed for the day

That's it. Those 5 data points give me a lot of useful information. They not only help me stay on track toward my writing goals, but they also show me areas that beg for improvement.

For example, I usually take it easy on Sundays. I might complete 2 or 3 short time chunks before calling it quits for the day. I can normally write 350 to 400 words in 25 minutes. But I noticed a few months ago that my output had slowed considerably during my Sunday time chunks. I was logging less than 250 words for each one.

My tracking spreadsheet revealed this problem. Being aware of it was enough to spur me to work faster.

That's why you need to track your progress.

We've covered a lot of ideas in this step. The time we've spent doing so has been a good investment. Your sleep schedule, exercise routine, diet and stress levels dramatically influence your workflow. Adjusting them accordingly can set the stage for making major improvements to your productivity. Also, your willingness to set goals and track your progress will ensure that you keep moving forward toward accomplishing whatever you set out to do.

In the next step, we'll take a look at an often-neglected, but critical, aspect of maximizing your productivity: avoiding burnout.

Step 7

Take Preventative Measures
To Avoid Burnout

Take Preventative Measures
To Avoid Burnout

Taking consistent and measured steps toward a clearly-defined goal ensures forward-moving progress and minimizes the likelihood of burnout.

* * *

Burnout was once considered to be the result of stress. Experts believed that ever-increasing levels of stress in an individual's life eventually causes him to reach a point at which he no longer cares about his work.

Today, researchers are less inclined to chalk up burnout to stress alone. They now attribute the condition to a multitude of factors.

At work, inadequate compensation, a lack of control and repetition of tasks can contribute to it. At home, insufficient sleep, a poor diet and the absence of meaningful relationships can set the stage.

Some people are more prone to burnout than others due to certain personality traits. For example, individuals with Type A personalities often drive themselves to the point of mental and physical exhaustion by always being "on the go." Likewise, perfectionists drive themselves to exhaustion by spending inordinate amounts of time perfecting everything they do. Chronic pessimism has also been associated with burnout.

How Burnout Affects Your Productivity

When you feel burnt out, it's difficult to be productive, regardless of how vigilant you are with sticking to your time chunks.

Your energy levels plummet, making you feel lethargic. Your immune system suffers, exposing you to a greater risk of sickness. You also feel less inclined to spend time with your friends and family members. Time spent alone can lead to increasing feelings of pessimism and even depression.

Even if you manage to work for 25 minutes (or whatever duration you choose for your time chunks), you won't be able to focus on your work. You'll need more time to complete any given task. If you run a blog and it normally takes you 4 time chunks to write and edit a blog post, doing so might now require 5 or 6 time chunks.

The worst thing about burnout is that it doesn't resolve itself. It continues to impair your productivity until you actively do something about it. We'll take a look at several ways you can do that in a few moments. First, let's talk about the differences between stress and burnout.

Stress Versus Burnout:
Are They The Same Thing?

Thanks in part to the psychology profession, which previously thought burnout is almost always caused by stress, many people still believe the two elements are inextricably linked. Some even believe they represent the same thing: they believe burnout is an extreme form of stress.

That misconception obfuscates the root causes of burnout. That, in turn, prevents the affected individual from identifying those causes and taking steps to resolve them.

So it's worth making a few distinctions between stress and burnout.

When a person is stressed, he feels a perpetual sense of urgency. For example, he might worry about tough-to-meet deadlines that follow him like a black cloud. When a person is burnt out, he doesn't have that same sense of urgency. Instead, he doesn't feel like doing anything. If there are deadlines to meet, he considers them low priorities.

When someone is stressed, they feel anxious. They have a nervous energy that drives them to take action, even if they're unsure what action they should take. When someone is burnt out, they lack energy, and therefore lack the motivation to take action.

While stress is a psychological response to stimuli, most of its effects are physical. Digestive problems, skin disorders and a greater susceptibility to heart disease are among its most common side effects.

Burnout is different. Its effects are predominantly emotional. You feel apathetic and helpless. You lack motivation and enjoyment in your work. You develop a pessimistic outlook. And because your work suffers, you feel a gnawing sense of dissatisfaction and failure.

Those are significant problems to overcome while using the time chunking method. So, let's take a look at ways to avoid burnout and stay engaged with your work.

Adopt Healthy Lifestyle Habits

In Step 6, we discussed the importance of sleep, exercise and diet with respect to how each affects your long-term use of the time chunking method. Collectively, they also play a major role in preventing burnout.

You need sufficient sleep each night to have the mental resources to cope with the challenges you'll face the following day.

You need to regularly exercise to keep your stress levels in check (not to mention stay fit).

You need to eat nutritious foods to give your mind the energy it needs to concentrate for extended periods without suffering mental fatigue. Eating healthy will also help you to avoid the gas, bloating, constipation and abdominal discomfort most Americans tolerate on a daily basis.

If you're tired, apathetic and saddled with gut-related issues, you'll be far more susceptible to burnout than if you were well-rested, energetic and free of gastrointestinal distress.

Set Limits On The Amount Of Time You Work

Earlier, we talked about individuals with Type A personalities being more prone to burnout. The reason is because those folks are always on the go. They're always "on," forgoing time off because they feel a perpetual need to perform.

That psychology is understandable. It's tempting to keep working when you feel you've hit a groove. You don't want to quit because you'll sacrifice your momentum. That's a seductive predicament. It can also damage your ability to work productively over the long run.

How? Because you'll eventually reach the point of mental and physical exhaustion, just like someone with a Type A personality. That's burnout.

Avoid that problem by creating a work schedule for each day. Then, stick to that schedule, even if doing so means breaking your groove. Resist the temptation to work past your personal "quitting time."

You may occasionally find yourself in situations where you need to work longer hours than expected to meet a deadline. That's a planning problem. You either wasted time that should have been devoted to completing the task at hand or you underestimated the amount of time the task would take to complete.

Either way, it's important to figure out why the problem occurred, and then take steps to prevent it from occurring in the future.

Take "Real" Breaks

The 5-minute breaks that separate 25-minute time chunks (the duration commonly used by enthusiasts) seem to give you very little time to do anything worthwhile. But you'll be surprised by the variety of rewarding activities you can perform in the space of a few minutes. I'll give you a long list of them in Step 8.

But for now, let's focus on "real" breaks.

You may recall the modified time chunking schedule I'm using these days (I shared it with you in Step 3). Here it is so you don't have to backtrack for it:

- Work for 50 minutes
  - Take a 10-minute break
- Work for 50 minutes
  - Take a 10-minute break
- Work for 50 minutes
  - Take a 40-minute break
- Work for 50 minutes
  - Take a 10-minute break
- Work for 50 minutes
  - Take a 20-minute break
- Work for 50 minutes
  - Call it a night!

Ten minutes is still a short period of time. It's a welcome recess after working full-throttle for 50 minutes, but I don't consider that to be a "real" break. It certainly won't prevent burnout.

But take a look at the 40-minute break I reward myself with after the third time chunk. That's a *real* break. I use it to eat a meal, take a nap or enjoy a long walk. Sometimes I'll run to my local Starbucks for a quick iced Americano.

The point is that the longer break gives my brain a chance to relax. That's a critical part of avoiding burnout. Your brain needs time to rest and recuperate.

The lesson? Don't try to power through an entire day of time chunks taking no more than 5-minute or 10-minute breaks. Give your brain plenty of opportunities to recharge.

Set Aside Time For Vacations

The word vacation probably invokes images of relaxing on a pristine beach - preferably in the Caribbean - while people bring you delicious drinks with umbrellas in them. Those images may be immediately followed by the thought, "*I haven't the time nor money to take a 2-week vacation in the Caribbean right now!*"

And so the idea dies on the vine.

But taking a vacation doesn't necessarily mean unplugging for 2 weeks. Nor does it have to mean buying plane tickets, booking hotel rooms and spending thousands of dollars. It can be as simple as taking a day off to enjoy with your family. Or staying overnight in a quaint bed and breakfast with your spouse.

If you have the time and funds to unplug for 2 weeks and relax in the Caribbean, go for it! But it's unnecessary to prevent burnout. Taking a vacation as short as 1 or 2 days can do wonders for your productivity and mental health.

Make Sure Your Goals Are Realistic

Your goals define what you want to achieve in your life. But they can represent a double-edged sword. On the one hand, your goals provide you with a destination. You can only create a plan of action if you know where you want to end up. Whether you're establishing goals for your career, finances or family, they help you to design your future.

On the other hand, poorly-crafted goals do more harm than good. They not only destroy your confidence, but they also sabotage your efforts to create your desired future.

It's critical to establish goals that are realistic. They must be achievable to pose any value to your workflow and long-term performance.

For example, suppose you want to make a living as a novelist. You decide to write and launch 6 full-length novels next year. If you have a full-time job and multiple kids, that goal is likely to be unrealistic (though not impossible). Chasing it will set the stage for burnout.

Make sure that every goal you set is achievable within the time frame you allow yourself. That will help you to stay on course and avoid the frustration and stress that typically accompany unrealistic goals.

Unplug From Technology

Tablets, smartphones, Kindles, and even your clunky home PC… if you're like me, your gadgets make your life better. They allow you to conduct research for your clients' projects. They give you multiple ways (calls, texts, email, etc.) to communicate with your friends, family and acquaintances. Your Kindle or iPad allows you to curl up on your couch and lose yourself in a great novel.

Technology has become an irreplaceable part of our lives. The only way to completely disengage is to live off the grid. But that's an unappealing option. Few of us would want to live life without our gadgets.

Having said that, it's important to unplug on occasion. Turn your phone off, step away from your laptop and leave your iPad behind. Take a mini-vacation from your gadgets.

Why? Because it's possible to drown in technology. You become overly-connected to the point that it starts to become a liability to your productivity. Worse, it's not always easy to tell when it's happening.

Researchers claim that immersing yourself in your gadgets without taking a break exposes you to the following side effects:

- increasing stress levels
- loss of productivity due to multitasking
- poor sleep

- elevated risk of depression
- internet addiction
- loss of interpersonal skills

Do yourself a favor. Unplug. You don't have to go "cold turkey" for long periods. Start small by abandoning your gadgets for half a day, or even a few hours. Then, go without them for an entire weekend.

It's a little scary at first, especially if you're the type of person who texts throughout the day, answers your phone whenever it rings and constantly checks your email. But once you build that "muscle," you'll find that being away from your gadgets is surprisingly rewarding.

It will also help you boost your productivity. You'll feel more engaged each time you sit down to complete a time chunk.

Make Time For Family And Friends

Spending time with your family and friends can have a therapeutic effect. It can relieve your stress, improve your self-image and give you a sense of identity. Your family and friends are the people who are most likely to be in your corner when life gets rough. They're the ones who will support you when you're feeling burnt out and apathetic, and encourage you to push through your lethargy.

Yet, how often do you forgo spending time with the people in your life? If you're like me, you do it more often than you can justify. Sometimes, you do it to get more work done. Other times, you do it to relax after a hard day's work. The day has taken a mental - and even physical - toll on you. You'd rather watch your favorite television shows on Netflix than spend time interacting with your loved ones.

Later, you kick yourself because you know you made the wrong choice. Even the best episode of *Walking Dead* can't compare to the joy of spending time with the people you love.

If you have an opportunity to hang out with the folks in your life, take it. In fact, jump at it. You'll find that the time you invest not only strengthens those connections, but gives your brain an opportunity to recharge.

A relaxed mind is a more productive, efficient mind.

Add Variety To Your Daily Workflow

Boring work is the hardest work of all. It's also a well-known productivity killer.

A vast and growing body of research shows that bored employees feel disengaged from their work. That lack of engagement sets the stage for a higher incidence of mistakes, low-quality output and inefficient effort. That, in turn, can easily lead to apathy, general unhappiness and even early-stage depression.

You don't need me to tell you that those things can have a disastrous effect on your use of time chunks. If you're apathetic, unhappy and depressed, the time chunking method won't save your workflow.

So how do you keep boredom at bay? By adding variety to your day.

Let's go back to our novelist example. Spending the entire day writing one particular novel can become monotonous. Why not put the novel aside and spend time writing that short story you've been meaning to pen? Or spend a few time chunks strengthening your author platform. Write a blog post, update your social media accounts or plan an email sequence.

The key is to mix things up. Doing so gives your brain something new to work on. You'll feel more engaged, and consequently work more productively.

Learn To Say No

This is one of the best habits I've developed in my life. The willingness to say no when others ask for my time and attention is important to me for two reasons (I'll bet you can relate to both of them).

First, saying no gives me more time. Every hour that isn't sacrificed to responding to others' needs can be used for things that I consider to be important. I can use that time to get more work done, hang out with the people I love or read a good book.

Second, saying no trains other people. It sets their expectations. As a result, they're less likely to approach me for help.

That may seem mean-spirited. But here's something I've learned in 9 out of 10 cases in which someone asks me for help...

The individual can easily resolve their "problem" on their own.

Let me give you an example. When I was in college, I drove a pickup truck. Friends - and even people I didn't know well - would constantly ask me to help them move. Relocating someone takes a lot of time. It's also hard labor, which I'm naturally averse to. But I would say yes because I thought it was the right thing to do.

I was wrong.

Just like putting a bowl of milk on your porch for a stray cat guarantees he'll keep stopping by, offering my truck and labor guaranteed I'd keep receiving requests for help.

So I learned to say no.

It was tough at first because I was battling the expectation I had previously established by always saying yes. But eventually, the old expectation was replaced with a new one: *Damon won't help you move. So don't bother asking him.*

Can you guess the result? I was asked less and less frequently. Finally, the requests vanished completely.

Mission accomplished. I had more time to study (remember, I was in college at the time), hang out with friends and build a side business. I was more productive, and thus happier.

If you find yourself always saying yes to people when they ask for your time, I strongly recommend saying no a few times. Give it a try. See how it feels. You'll discover that setting boundaries for others will reduce your stress, prevent burnout and ultimately improve your life.

You'll be regaining control of the most valuable asset you have at your disposal: your time.

This part of the action guide is dense for good reason. We had a lot of important things to cover regarding how to avoid burnout while using the time chunking method. I guarantee that incorporating the above suggestions in your life will make you far more productive.

In Step 8, we're going to switch gears and discuss the variety of activities you can do on your breaks. You'll have already considered many of them. Some, however, might surprise you...

Step 8

Create A Master List Of Things To Do During Breaks

Create A Master List Of Things To Do During Breaks

A 5-minute break is plenty of time to complete small tasks that are littering your to-do list.

* * *

You've worked hard for 25 minutes and you're ready to take a short break. The problem is, the typical time chunking method only gives you 5 minutes. And there aren't many things you can do in 5 minutes, right?

Wrong.

There are a myriad of activities you can do during your short breaks. The key is to brainstorm and create a list ahead of time. That way, you can avoid wasting precious minutes coming up with things to do. Instead, you can hit the ground running and make the most of your breaks.

This step is going to be relatively short (unlike Step 7). We're going to breeze through many of the simple things you can do during your 5-minute breaks. These are activities that I have on the list that sits next to my workstation. Look through them and add the ones you think you might enjoy to your own list.

Most of the activities you'll find below are geared toward folks who work from home. It's also worth noting that we're talking about small tasks. You're not going to be able to mow your front lawn or get your grocery shopping done for the week.

But you *will* be able to do any of the following:

Use the bathroom.

When nature calls, it's important to respond. Having said that, try to avoid disrupting the work segment of your time chunks to answer the call. Instead, use the bathroom during your break.

Take your dog for a walk.

Your dog needs to answer nature's call too. The problem is, unless he has access to a doggy door, he'll need your help. When break time arrives, grab his leash and take him outside. The short walk will do double-duty since it will give you an opportunity to stretch your legs.

Make a pot of coffee for yourself.

Studies show that moderate amounts of caffeine can boost your productivity. If your stomach can tolerate coffee, use your 5-minute break to brew a pot for yourself. If you have a sensitive gut, make a cup of black tea. It will give you a subtle booster shot of caffeine without the GI distress.

Start a load of laundry.

Those dirty clothes and towels aren't going to clean themselves. When you're ready to take a break, throw a load into your washer or transfer a load from your washer to your dryer. Doing so forces you to get up from your desk and move your body.

As a bonus, you'll have clean clothes to wear.

Stretch your legs and grab a glass of water.

If you don't feel like doing something constructive with your time, just get up and grab a glass of water. Being productive requires staying hydrated. As an alternative, you could keep a huge water bottle at your desk. But you'd be robbing yourself of the opportunity to stretch your legs.

Perform a few simple exercises.

If you're like me, you've probably told yourself on countless occasions that you don't have time to exercise. You may have even convinced yourself. The reality is that you can do a number of simple routines during your 5-minute breaks. Here are a few ideas:

- push-ups
- sit-ups
- squats
- kettlebell raises
- yoga
- hip thrusts
- planks
- lunges
- jump rope

Declutter your desk.

According to experts, a cluttered desk reveals a cluttered mind. Personally, I find comfort in Albert Einstein's remark that "*If a cluttered desk is a sign of a cluttered mind, of what, then, is an empty desk a sign?*"

Working amidst chaos can be beneficial for some people. Clutter seems to spur their creativity. The jury is still out on whether that same clutter actually improves their productivity.

Here's what I recommend: if you find yourself constantly looking for things on your desk, it's time to tidy things up. The good news is that you can declutter your desk during one or two short breaks. The only requirement is that you're ruthless about what you decide to toss out. Now is not the time to be sentimental.

Practice breathing exercises.

Most of us are accustomed to taking shallow breaths. We sit at our desks, slumped over our keyboards, maintaining a posture that encourages the habit. Unfortunately, shallow breathing comes with a host of adverse health effects.

For example, it limits the amount of oxygen that reaches the brain, making it harder to focus. It increases our susceptibility to higher stress levels, further impairing our ability to work productively. It can even prevent us from getting the restful sleep we need each night.

Use your 5-minute breaks to practice deep breathing exercises. You'll feel more relaxed and alert. As a result, you'll be more productive during the work segments of your time chunks.

Pick a few items in your closet to discard.

Closets have a way of becoming packed with unnecessary clothes, shoes and sundry household items. We buy new clothes without discarding old ones. We stuff items in our closets that don't see the light of day for years.

Why not use your 5-minute breaks to clean out your closets? Don't worry about cleaning them out completely. Just pick a few items to toss out or donate to Goodwill. Be ruthless. If you haven't worn the ugly sweater hanging in the back of your closet since 2010, what are the chances you'll wear it this year?

Wash the dishes sitting in your sink (or load the dishwasher).

Dishes have a way of piling up in the sink if you don't wash them. Strangely, they refuse to wash themselves. Unless you're allowing weeks to go by without washing your dishes, plates and glasses, you should be able to clear out your sink within few minutes.

That's perfect for a break following a time chunk!

Make reservations for dinner.

My wife and I go out to dinner every Friday. It gives us a chance to unplug from work and enjoy each other's company while scarfing down delicious food. But because Fridays are busy at the restaurants we frequent, we only visit those that accept reservations.

Some restaurants take reservations online. Others will only take them by phone. Either way, it only takes a few minutes to make them. That makes the task a perfect fit for a time chunking break.

Open your (snail) mail.

Most of the mail I receive is advertising. My bills are delivered and paid online. Personal correspondence is handled via email and phone (does anyone still send letters?).

But after a week, there are usually at least a few items sitting in my mailbox. I can easily open them and discard the junk within five minutes.

Note that when I say "mail," I'm talking about the kind that's delivered by postal workers. I'm not referring to email. We'll talk briefly about email in the section titled "A Few Things To Avoid Doing During Your Breaks."

Listen to your favorite song.

Music helps us to disconnect from our work. It gives the brain a break. Studies show that it can also stimulate physiological effects. Researchers have found that music can affect our blood pressure, alter our mood and even boost the secretion of select immune hormones. They claim it can also improve our spatial reasoning and reading skills.

Having said that, the type of music you listen to plays a role. The effects of listening to Chopin and Mozart are likely to differ from the effects of listening to Metallica and Eminem.

The research is beyond the scope of this action guide. The point is that five minutes is plenty of time to give your brain a musical break between your time chunks.

Play a video game.

Video games can provide the same healthy disconnect from your work as music. The difference is that your mind remains active. Most video games involve achieving an objective that requires skill or concentration (often both). Mental engagement is a corequisite.

According to the American Psychological Association (APA), playing video games boosts our problem-solving skills. That's worth considering if you routinely face complex challenges during the course of your workday. Playing games can also improve our neural processing and ability to focus.

Gaming may not be the complete waste of time that many people seem to think.

There's an important caveat to bear in mind if you plan to play video games: choose games that are played in stages that can be completed in a few minutes.

A great example is the popular game Quell. Not only does it offer gorgeous graphics, but it's played as a series of levels, each of which can be completed in 60 seconds or less. Moreover, the game's format is that of a puzzle, which keeps your mind engaged. If you have a smartphone or tablet, you can download the game for free (Amazon) or a couple dollars (iTunes).

Other good games include Free Word Wrap, Hangman, Monster Busters, Retro Attack and Solitaire. The trait they share is that they can be played quickly without pulling you into a multi-hour gaming session like Halo or Call of Duty. Hundreds of similar video games can be downloaded to your smartphone for free or played directly through your browser.

Stare outside.

Have you ever walked outside after a hard work session and stared off into the distance? Gazing absently at distant trees, clouds or a calm body of water can be absolutely mesmerizing. Even sitting on the porch and watching cars pass by can have an almost hypnotic effect.

It's a great way to spend a break between time chunks! It gives your mind an opportunity to relax and release stress.

A quick tip: keep a timer with you. Otherwise, it's too easy to be lulled into hypnotic complacency.

Pay a few bills.

Ideally, you'll have automatic bill payments set up online so you can avoid spending time paying them manually. If you don't have your bills on auto-pay, use your breaks to take care of them. Five minutes is plenty of time if you're organized.

If you pay your bills online, create a folder in your browser with bookmarks for each vendor's site. When you're ready to take a break, simply open the bookmarks and pay your bills. There's no need to open snail mail invoices since each vendor's site will display the amount due.

If you're still writing checks, you'll need to work fast.

Opening snail mail, writing checks and licking stamps takes time. Depending on how many bills you have to pay, five minutes may not be enough. Now's a great time to make the switch to paying them online.

Play your guitar (or keyboard or violin or…).

If you play a musical instrument, use your breaks between time chunks to practice. Doing so allows you to keep your mind and body engaged while enjoying a healthy mental disconnect from the task at hand. In addition, you'll improve your skill on your preferred instrument.

It goes without saying that now isn't the time to perfect that Rachmaninoff prelude in C-sharp minor. Save that task for your longer breaks (or better yet, after you've called it a day). Instead, use the short break to practice scales. Or fine-tune that killer riff or captivating melody you've been working on.

Clean a small section of your house.

Few people look forward to cleaning their homes. Vacuuming, dusting, mopping and sweeping hold zero excitement for most of us. If you're like me, you love living in a clean house, but are allergic to the tasks that make it possible.

My problem is that the job seems so huge. Cleaning everything can take hours. That's discouraging to the point that it's easier to avoid doing it. I know that's not a solution, but my natural aversion to chores helps me to rationalize the decision.

There's a better solution that's been working for me lately:

I use my breaks between time chunks to handle chores. Before my first time chunk of the day, I'll put the vacuum cleaner, dusting rag, indoor broom and dishwashing detergent in a place that's easy to access. That way, I don't have to search for them. When I'm ready to take break, I clean a small section of my house.

I might vacuum a room, wash last night's dishes or mop the bathroom floor. I work fast because I don't want to spend a lot of time. I'm not striving for perfection. My house will never make the cover of Architectural Digest or House Beautiful. My goal is to keep it clean it, but work quickly.

If your house needs to be cleaned and you don't want to hire a maid service, try doing your chores during your breaks. The key is to plan them ahead of time. Identify the sections of your house that you'll address during each break. Then, retrieve the necessary cleaning supplies so they'll be ready when you need them.

Declutter the inside of your car.

When I was in college, the cabin of my truck was an absolute mess. (Unless I was going out on a date. Then, miraculously, my truck was clean as a whistle.) Things are different these days. The interior of my car is always clean.

Here's my secret:

First, I'm a minimalist by nature. I tend to avoid collecting things, so there's rarely junk laying around in my car.

Second, when there are items that need to be discarded (for example, a leftover Starbucks cup in the cupholder), I toss them during my breaks.

I encourage you to do the same if your car is cluttered. Unless you've been collecting junk for months, you should be able to declutter the interior within minutes. Most of the stuff can probably be thrown out.

Make your bed.

If you hate making the bed, I sympathize. It's not on my list of favorite activities either. But since my wife and I love getting into a made bed, it needs to get made at some point.

This is another task that's best left for a short break. I can walk away from my desk after a time chunk, and move my body and get my blood circulating in the process.

Don't make your bed the moment you get up in the morning (unless that makes you feel more organized and thus more productive). Wait until you're ready to take a short break during the workday.

Organize drawers and cabinets.

If you're one of those rare individuals whose drawers and cabinets are always organized, I salute you. That's worthy of a commendation.

My drawers and cabinets have a mind of their own. I can organize them on Monday and find them in complete disarray by Friday. The problem is that my wife and I have too many items stored away in them. My sock drawer has too many socks. The dish cabinet has too many dishes. We have so many forks and knives that a starved army can visit our house and never want for utensils.

Lately, I've managed to deal with the issue by spending a few minutes here and there organizing things. It's no longer a losing battle. I no longer open my kitchen cabinets and resign myself to surrendering to the chaos. I can actually find the items I need.

You've probably guessed that I organize the drawers and cabinets in my house during my breaks between time chunks. And you'd be right. If yours are a mess, give my strategy a try. As with cleaning your house, plan which drawers and cabinets you'll attack in advance.

Visit your favorite joke site.

Jokes can provide a much-needed break from the intense focus you've maintained during your time chunks. They allow you to disconnect from your work, giving your brain a chance to recuperate. You might be surprised by the effect a few laughs can have on your outlook after 25 minutes of hard concentration.

As you know, there's no shortage of joke sites online. But I can count the number of good ones on a single hand (and have 3 fingers left over). Personally, I like JumboJoke.com. It's run by a gentleman named Randy Cassingham, who also runs the longstanding "odd news" site ThisIsTrue.com. Here's why I like the site:

- the jokes are short
- most of the jokes are pretty good
- although some of the jokes deal with risque material, none are "dirty"

- you can drill down to various categories
- the site is regularly updated

If you have a favorite joke site, definitely use it. If not, check out JumboJoke.com.

Read your favorite comic strips.

Comic strips serve the same purpose as joke sites. They give you an opportunity to disconnect from your work by stimulating your funny bone. Plus, you're not investing yourself into an activity that might take longer than 5 minutes. You can read several strips during a short break.

I'm a long-time fan of comic strips. A strip writer's ability to deliver a chuckle - and sometimes an outright guffaw - using little more than a few images and words fascinates me. I wish I had that talent. Here are a few of my favorites:

- Dilbert
- Calvin & Hobbes
- Andy Capp
- Ballard Street
- Doonesbury
- Bloom County

You'll find a ton of strips archived at GoComics.com. I have a folder in my Chrome browser with links to my favorite ones. That way, I don't have to look for them. I just open the folder, click "Open All Bookmarks" and blast through all of them in less than 5 minutes.

Review your short-term and long-term goals.

You should have goals that detail what you'd like to accomplish over the next few months and years. It's not enough to keep them in your head. You need to write them down. Writing your goals down gives them clarity. It transforms them from ambiguous desires to clear-cut objectives. That's why so many successful entrepreneurs and business owners write down their goals. (Some even keep them on a piece of paper in their wallets.)

Writing down your goals gives you an opportunity to review them, a task that's perfectly-suited for breaks between time chunks. You can do it in a few minutes.

Periodically reviewing your goals is important because it helps you to monitor your progress. If you've created an effective goal-setting and tracking system, you'll be able to see at a glance if you're on track to accomplish the things you've set out to do. You'll also be able to identify goals that have become less important to you over time. Assign them a lower priority.

Use a couple of your breaks each week to assess your goals and gauge your progress toward accomplishing them. Go through your list and ask yourself whether each one is still important to you. If it is, verify that you're still on track given the deadline you assigned to it.

Identify small tasks on your to-do list, and complete them.

Way back in Step 2, we talked about batch processing. It's the practice of setting aside a block of time (for example, 25 minutes) to work on a pool of small tasks. By devoting a block of time to them, you can complete a greater number of them in an organized fashion than would be possible by addressing them sporadically.

In short, it works.

If you're like me, you have a huge list of small items that need to be handled at some point. For example, here's a snapshot of some of the tasks on my master "to do" list:

- choose an abdominal exercise
- buy the "Perfect Health Diet" by Paul Jaminet
- create a Van Halen playlist in Grooveshark
- pay car insurance
- take a look at the "Clutterless" Wordpress theme
- print calendars for 1st quarter of the year
- find out how much fiber is in a sweet potato

Notice how each item can be completed in a minute or less? I can knock several of them out in a single 10-minute break (remember, I follow a modified time chunking schedule). These type of items are important to me, but they can quickly add up and make my "to do" list seem absolutely frightening.

I can stem the tide by working on them during my breaks.

A Few Things To Avoid
Doing During Your Breaks

Thus far, we've focused on activities that are well-suited for 5-minute breaks. All of them can be done without fear of accidentally extending your breaks. Let's now talk about activities you should refrain from doing - at least until you have more time at your disposal.

Don't check email. It's too easy to become immersed in it. You might intend to spend 5 minutes replying to clients, friends and family only to discover that 20 minutes have evaporated. Wait until your lunch break or the end of the day to return emails.

Social media is even more seductive than email. You've probably experienced firsthand how it can destroy your productivity and derail your time chunks. Save it for later.

YouTube can be a huge problem for those of us who are curious. If I listen to a single ZZ Top song, you can be sure I'll look up their albums and concerts, and maybe even read their Wikipedia page. YouTube is like a drug for me. If you're the same way, I strongly suggest avoiding the site during your 5-minute breaks.

News sites are just as bad as YouTube. The headlines are expertly crafted to get you to click through and read the stories. Then, off to the side of the page, you'll see a bunch of other tantalizing headlines. It's like falling down the proverbial rabbit hole. Save the news for later. Or better yet, go on a low-information diet and skip it entirely. When was the last time you read a news item that actually improved your life?

Don't return phone calls. It's too easy to become trapped in a conversation that extends your short breaks. Remember, you're the only one who has an incentive to protect your time. So protect it ruthlessly.

Think twice before checking your favorite blogs and forums. If you're just planning to read a short post, you may be fine. But if you're going to leave a comment or post a response, you're asking for trouble. You know as well as I do that if someone disagrees with your comment or response, you're going to be tempted to defend yourself. It's natural. It's also a huge time waster.

I speak from experience.

Avoid interactions that require deep, intense thinking. Your breaks are intended to give your mind a rest. That way, you can come back to your work feeling mentally refreshed and ready to complete another time chunk. If you apply yourself to a complex problem, your brain will never receive its needed break. Leave the heavy stuff for the evening, after you've turned your computer off for the day.

Remember when I said Step 8 would be a short one? Apparently, I lied. It ended up a lot longer than I thought it would. My apologies. The upside is that you now have a long list of activities you can do during your breaks between time chunks. If you're lacking for ideas, use the ones I've outlined above.

In the next step, we're going to take a look at tools that may help you squeeze even more value from the time chunking method.

Step 9

Expand Your Toolset To Optimize Your Use Of The Time Chunking Method

Expand Your Toolset To Optimize Your Use Of The Time Chunking Method

Numerous phone apps, software applications and services are available to help you leverage the time chunking method.

* * *

I'm a Luddite when it comes to gadgets and apps. I prefer my dumb phone to a smartphone. I prefer paper and pen to the myriad online apps that offer to help me organize my time, thoughts and projects. And I prefer an old-fashioned timer to an online timer for keeping me on task during my time chunks.

Having said that, I realize that arguing against the use of technology with respect to the time chunking method is akin to tilting at windmills. Not only are there countless productivity apps and tools available, but the number seems to be growing exponentially. That being the case, I'm going to cover several of them in this step.

You'll notice that many of the tools I cover below do the same thing, but offer a different interface and visual presentation. Some also offer additional bells and whistles you might find useful. I'll try to hit the most salient features of each so you can choose the tools that best complement your workflow and style preferences.

Let's start off with a couple caveats:

Caveat #1:

The apps and tools covered below are only a small subset of the thousands that are out there. There's no way I can create an exhaustive list because the list grows each day. That would be an unwinnable war.

Caveat #2:

I haven't used most of the apps and tools covered below. Again, I'm a Luddite. I like simple systems, or at least systems that can be implemented effectively without relying on a variety of apps. I also like showing folks how to squeeze more out of their day. That's what this action guide is about. The more time I spend tinkering with unnecessary productivity apps, the less time I have available to actually produce training materials that provide long-term value.

So, where does that leave us? Here's my advice:

Use the following list as a resource for generating *ideas* on how to get more out of the time chunking method. In other words, focus less on each tool's "coolness factors" and more on how its features might help you achieve more during the course of each day.

For example, consider the app at RememberTheMilk.com. It's essentially a tool for managing items on your to-do list. It's not the only such tool out there. More to the point, it will likely evolve into something more robust over time or eventually be overshadowed by superior tools that meet similar needs.

Rather than focusing on how great a tool RTM is - in my opinion, it is great - think about how it's designed to meet a specific need: managing to-do items. It allows you to use tags, schedule reminders and even collaborate with others. Now, think about how those particular features might boost your productivity.

I guarantee that next year we'll see a slew of new apps and programs that outshine those that are available today. Don't worry about implementing the best of the lot. Again, that's an unwinnable war.

Enough specious claptrap. Let's get started.

Google Timer

Here's how to access it. Visit Google.com and type in "timer 25 minutes." Google will display a timer with 25 minutes on the clock at the top of its search results. It will start counting down automatically.

I love the Google Timer for a few reasons. First, it's free. Second, it doesn't require installing a new app; you can use it directly through your browser on Google.com. Third, it's the perfect complement for the time chunking method when you're not at home - at least for me.

I do a considerable amount of work at coffee shops like Starbucks and It's A Grind (a local chain based in Southern California). In that setting, using an old-fashioned kitchen timer would be inappropriate since it would disturb others. The Google Timer is a great alternative. I usually listen to instrumental music through my laptop while working, so I always have earbuds in my ears. The Google Timer's alert is loud enough to cut through the music without being overly-abrasive.

It's perfect (for me). By the way, did I mention that it's free?

Requirements: works through your browser.

Marinara Timer

Marinara Timer is designed to support folks who use the time chunking method. It's an online app, so there's nothing to download or install. Access it for free by visiting MarinaraTimer.com.

It comes with 3 modes. The first mode supports a traditional approach to time chunking - 25 minutes followed by a 5-minute break. After the fourth time chunk, the app gives you a 15-minutes break.

The second mode, called Marinara, allows you to adjust the time intervals. You can assign different lengths of time for each session, work or break. This is the mode I recommend since you can personalize your time chunks to complement your workflow.

The third mode, called Kitchen Timer, is self-explanatory. You essentially choose a length of time and the timer starts to count down, similar to the Google Timer (see above). It's great for timeboxing, but less adaptable to the time chunking method.

Requirements: works through your browser.

Remember The Milk

We talked briefly about Remember The Milk above, but it's worth highlighting a few of its features as they pertain to your time chunks.

RTM is essentially a task management app. But don't dismiss it as a mere alternative to pen and paper. It's powerful and versatile, and offers a lot of useful features. But it's also simple to use. That's a huge advantage in my book.

So what does it do? If you're a "Getting Things Done" (GTD) enthusiast, you'll love that it supports unlimited lists. Those lists can be tagged for easy identification. You can also create tabs to help you organize your lists according to priority. Items on your to-do lists can be assigned due dates or left alone. You can also schedule tasks that need to be done on a recurring basis (for example, paying your cable bill).

It does a lot more, of course. Visit RememberTheMilk.com to check it out.

It's free. You can also upgrade to a Pro account ($25 per year at the time of writing) to gain access to a raft of extra features. Try the free version first.

Requirements: Works through your browser. Also integrates with your smartphone or tablet (Android or Mac/iOS).

Stayfocusd

A lot of apps are designed to block your access to sites so you can avoid the distraction they pose to your time chunks. Stayfocusd is based on the same principle, but gives you more flexibility with regard to how you decide to use your time.

The idea is that you have a number of non-productive tasks that you enjoy doing. Ideally, you'd do them during your breaks or later in the evening, after you've called it a day. But if you find yourself getting distracted by the endless array of infotainment options online, Stayfocusd will help you stay on track.

It allows you to add sites and pages to a "Blocked Sites" list. (As an alternative, you can choose to block *all* sites except for those you add to an "Allowed Sites" list). Then, you set an amount of time that you'll allow yourself to access those sites during the course of a single day.

The timer will either start counting down immediately or at a time you choose. Once the amount of time you've chosen elapses, Stayfocusd blocks your access.

It's easy to cheat when using these types of apps. You can go into their settings pages and disable them, allowing yourself to access your blocked sites and ignore your work. The folks who designed Stayfocusd included a "Nuclear Option" to solve that problem. If enabled, it hides the extension in your browser (Chrome). You are thus prevented from accessing the settings page that day and disabling it.

Stayfocusd is free and can be installed from the Chrome Web Store.

Requirements: Chrome browser. Works on Windows, Mac OS or Chrome OS (on Chromebooks).

Toodledo

Toodledo is a perfect complement to the Getting Things Done system. It's an online task management tool on steroids. You can create to-do lists, prioritize the items on those lists and share them with others. You can schedule tasks, set reminders and view everything you need to get done on a customizable calendar. You can also outline projects, take notes and monitor your progress from an easy-to-use interface.

I'm only scratching the surface. Toodledo can do a ton of useful things, many of which will appeal to you if you're a GTD fan and like using online productivity tools. A friend of mine has used Toodledo for years and loves it. But I'll admit, he lost me while describing the litany of features it offers (remember, I'm a kitchen timer and pen and paper type of guy).

Toodledo is a "freemium" app. That means you can use it for free or pay a monthly premium to access an array of extra features. If you decide to pay for the upgrade, you can cancel it at any time.

Access it at Toodledo.com.

Requirements: Works through your browser. Also integrates with your smartphone or tablet (Android or Mac/iOS).

IQTell

Here's another app that GTD enthusiasts will love. IQTell aims to help you be more productive while simultaneously helping you to keep your email inbox under control. The way it accomplishes that feat is impressive, even to to a self-professed Luddite like myself.

First, IQTell can grab your incoming email from multiple services and display them in a single list. Suppose you have a Gmail account for personal use, a work-related email account and a Yahoo email account for merchant offers. IQTell can pull them into its own interface, making it easy for you to handle all of your email without logging into various platforms.

Second, you can create unlimited to-do lists, set reminders, milestones and deadlines for tasks, and attach tags for better organization. IQTell also integrates with Evernote (one of my favorite tools, which we'll talk about later).

There's a lot to like about this app. Although I'm not a huge GTD fan, I'm tempted to try it. Like Toodledo, it's a freemium. You can register an account for free and upgrade to take advantage of extra features. Note that syncing between your email accounts, calendars and contact lists is available with a free account, but only for 60 days (at the time of writing). After that period elapses, the syncing feature goes away unless you upgrade.

Access it at IQTell.com.

Requirements: Works through your browser. Also integrates with your smartphone or tablet (Android or Mac/iOS).

Omnifocus

Omnifocus aims to keep your life in order. It's another GTD-inspired app that focuses on helping you manage your to-do lists.

Although its mission is relatively simple, its execution is complex. Omnifocus tries to separate tasks that are related to different areas in your life and help you to manage them without getting lost in the details. That's an ambitious goal.

You can set up projects and create tasks under each area. The visual presentation of those projects and tasks is similar to Evernote's organizational scheme. You can also apply filters to your lists, allowing you to drill down to the tasks that you consider priorities at any given time. Omnifocus also offers a location proximity feature that notifies you about to-do tasks related to stores and other destinations you're near.

The app seems to have a steep learning curve. If you intend to try it, realize that before jumping in. Otherwise, be prepared to feel frustrated.

Omnifocus is designed to be used in the Mac universe. Hence, you can access it on your iPhone, iPad or Macbook Air or Pro (or any other Mac computer). Unfortunately, it's not free. The price varies by device. The least costly option is for the iPhone. The iPad version costs a bit more. The Mac versions - it comes in Standard and Pro - are even more expensive.

Download Omnifocus from Omnigroup.com or the iTunes App store.

Requirements: Mac OS (iPhone, iPad, etc.).

Pomio

If you have an iPhone or iPad and you're looking for an app that does a lot more than just offer a simple countdown timer, you'll like Pomio. In addition to a timer, it allows you to create projects and to-do lists, color-code items and create time chunks for each task (or batch of tasks).

Pomio doesn't force you to use a conventional 25-minute work segment. You can set it for any length of time you desire. You can also customize the duration of your breaks. That's a huge benefit if you're following a modified time chunking schedule, as I recommended in Step 3.

Pomio also comes with tracking tools. For example, you can check, at a glance, how many time chunks you've completed over a given period. That will indicate if you need to log more time at work each day - e.g. an extra time chunk - to get things done.

Pomio isn't free. It costs $2.99 (it's sometimes offered at a discount). Download it from the iTunes App store.

Requirements: Mac iOS (iPhone or iPad).

Promodoro

Promodoro is designed for those who own iPhones and iPads. It's easy to use thanks to an intuitive interface. You can customize the length of time you'd like to work without distraction. You can also customize the duration of your breaks.

Promodoro will alert you via an audible alarm when your work segments and breaks are over (you can turn this feature off). It will do so even if you turn your phone or iPad off. The app will also keep track of your time chunks so you can evaluate your progress and measure it against a baseline.

Promodoro costs $0.99 (at the time of writing). Download it from the iTunes App store.

Requirements: Mac iOS (iPhone or iPad).

Focus Time

The first thing you'll notice about Focus Time is its beautiful, polished interface. Brash visuals and bright colors - e.g. yellow, red and green - reflect your progress during each time chunk. In addition, you can see how many time chunks you've completed during the day directly underneath the countdown interface. It's much more than just a countdown timer.

Focus Time gives you the flexibility to adjust your work segments and breaks to complement your workflow. It also lets you choose from a selection of sounds to notify you when your work segments and breaks are over.

Focus Time costs $4.99 (at the time of writing). Download it from the iTunes App store.

One quick note: don't confuse this app with "It's Focus Time!" The latter is a different product. It hasn't been updated in awhile, and thus I've chosen to not include it on this list.

Requirements: Mac iOS (iPhone or iPad).

Pomodroido

Here's a free app designed for Android devices. Pomodroido doesn't try to match the versatility of other time management and productivity tools. It's a simple app that helps you to stick to the traditional 25-minutes-of-work-followed-by-a-5-minute break routine.

Unfortunately, development has stalled. But given that it's free, simple and available for Android users, I thought it would be a good idea to include it. A pro version is available for $2.99, but it doesn't seem to offer much more than the free version. If you'd like to reward the developer for creating the app, buying the Pro version is a great way to do so.

Download both versions - free or Pro - from the Google Play store.

Requirements: Android phone or tablet.

PomodoroApp (TeamViz)

As its name implies, PomodoroApp is yet another tool that aims to keep you focused and productive during your workday. It not only includes a configurable timer, but also offers several notification options. In addition, you can create calendars that give you a useful bird's-eye view of your projects and tasks. Visually-appealing graphs will show you how many time chunks you've completed each day.

PomodoroApp is a freemium app. A "lite" version is available for free. A "professional" version is available for a small monthly fee ($1.99 per month). If you run a business with several employees, you can opt for a "company" version. It offers more bells and whistles. It also comes with a much bigger monthly fee ($49 per month).

A couple of quick notes:

First, the developers have noted that they've changed the name of their app to TeamViz due to legal issues. That rebranding process is still ongoing. For that reason, I've used its original name.

Second, there is another app called PomodoroApp that is available through the iTunes App store. As far as I can tell, it has no affiliation to the tool created by the TeamViz developers. The remarks I've made above are exclusively for the TeamViz tool.

Download the PomodoroApp/TeamViz tool from

TeamViz.com or the iTunes App store or Google Play store.

Requirements: integrates with your smartphone or tablet (Android or Mac/iOS).

Eggscellent

Just in case you need yet another time management tool for your Mac, let me to introduce you to Eggscellent. It's a timer and to-do list manager wrapped up in a glossy package. But it goes much further, allowing you to sync and integrate your Omnifocus account (we covered Omnifocus above).

Having said the above, the feature that makes Eggscellent stand out is its visual presentation. When you start a time chunk, a graphic appears on your computer screen displaying an unripe tomato. As your time chunk progresses, the tomato ripens and eventually falls off its vine.

It's clear the developers put a lot of work into creating their app. Their efforts paid off. If you love visuals, you'll love this tool. Download it from Eggscellent.com or the Mac App store. It used to cost $4.99, but it now available for free.

Requirements: Mac with OS X 10.6.6 or higher.

Evernote

I love Evernote. It's one of my favorite online tools. When I first started using it years ago, I was clueless regarding its potential. I used it like many people still do: to create to-do lists and capture random notes for future reference. Since then, I've learned to harness it and use it more effectively. As such, it now plays a much bigger role in my daily productivity.

What can you do with Evernote? A ton of things. Keep track of important, easy-to-forget details, such as your mechanic's phone number, your medical records and Department of Motor Vehicles information. Install Evernote's Web Clipper app and save articles for later reference (it's better than bookmarking the articles). If you're a novelist, keep track of your story ideas and flesh them out over time.

I'm just scratching the surface, of course. Entire books have been written on how to squeeze maximum value out of Evernote. (I plan to write one geared specifically to those who want to use the platform to be more productive.)

If you're not already using Evernote, I strongly encourage you to register an account. Don't worry about learning how to do everything. Start with the basics just to get accustomed to its interface. Create a few to-do lists. Play around with the tags. Create a few folders to organize your projects. Set a few reminders.

Evernote is a freemium product. The free version is excellent.

When you're ready to take advantage of Evernote's full potential - including working offline and the ability to annotate PDFs - upgrade to the Premium version. It's $5 a month.

Requirements: Works through your browser. Also integrates with your smartphone or tablet (Android or Mac/iOS).

Thoughts On Using Online Tools And Apps With Your Time Chunks

You may be thinking to yourself, "Wait a second. That's it?! Aren't there at least a few hundred more apps out there I can use?"

The answer, of course, is yes. But if that's what you're thinking, you might be addicted to productivity tools. One of the keys to successfully using the time chunking method in your daily workflow is to avoid getting bogged down in unnecessary extras.

Stick to the basics. For me, that means using an old-fashioned timer and keeping a spiral-bound notebook next to me to keep track of my to-do items. I strongly recommend that you start from the same place. If you need an extra tool to accomplish a specific goal, find and implement one that meets that need.

By starting from simplicity, you'll avoid wasting time playing around with an endless array of apps that will become obsolete when new apps arrive next year. The less time you waste, the more time you'll have to get things done. And that means you'll have more time to enjoy the people and things you consider important in your life (family, friends, hobbies, etc.).

Step 10

Stop Reading And Start Taking Control Of Your Time!

Stop Reading And Start Taking Control Of Your Time!

Information is useless without application. It's time to take action on what you've learned in this guide.

* * *

This step is arguably the most important of the lot. None of the information, tips and recommendations I've given you in this action guide will do you any good unless you apply them.

Earlier, I noted that "true learning comes with application." The only way to boost your productivity with the time chunking method is to put forth the effort to apply it to your daily workflow.

Doing so is simple. But that doesn't mean it's easy. Like forming any habit, implementing the time chunking method in your life is going to take repetition and diligence. You'll face resistance as your brain rebels against the restrictions you try to place on it. You have to retrain your brain and set new expectations with regard to the level of distraction you'll allow it to enjoy.

Many people who finish reading this action guide will think to themselves, "*The time chunking method will definitely help me get more work done! I'm going to do more research before I start using it.*"

My friend, let me encourage you to start today. You don't

need to do more research. I've given you a complete blueprint for implementing the time chunking method today.

Don't feel as if you need to make an immediate, comprehensive change to the manner in which you approach your work. Start with baby steps. Set aside a half-hour. Set a timer for 25 minutes and devote your attention to a single project. When your timer goes off, take a 5-minute break.

No matter how busy you are, you can perform a single time chunk. That alone will give you insight into whether it produces positive results for you. I'd be willing to bet that once you perform one time chunk, you'll want to perform another. And then another. Meanwhile, you'll find that you're better able to concentrate and get things done instead of being continuously distracted by Facebook, CNN.com and your favorite blogs.

Don't wait to start taking advantage of the time chunking method. Start using it today!

Final Thoughts On Leveraging The Time Chunking Method

Increasing your productivity is not a battle that can be won and forgotten. It's a constant struggle that demands your dedication and persistence. Left unchecked, your mind will always gravitate toward activities that offer instant gratification, no matter how ephemeral.

It would rather read Facebook and Twitter than work on that report your boss wants completed by the end of the week.

It would rather watch cat videos on YouTube than write that article you've been meaning to submit to that trade publication.

It would rather call a friend than deal with that frustrating website/server issue.

When it comes to work vs. play, the brain is like your dog. It will always prefer to play. Always. Your job is to implement rules that allow you to get your work done efficiently so you can play later. That's what the time chunking method will do for you.

The key is to stick with it, even if your brain tries to persuade you to do otherwise.

Using time chunks will dramatically change the way you work. It will catapult your productivity, so you'll have more time to do the things that make your life rewarding. It can even boost your creativity since you'll have more time to brainstorm ideas.

I speak from experience.

If you're dealing with resistance, ask yourself these 2 questions...

1. What do you have to lose by trying a quick time chunk right now?
2. What do you have to gain in the weeks, months and years to come by making the time chunking method a part of your daily process?

May I Ask You To Do Me A Small Favor?

If you enjoyed reading this action guide, would you please leave a short review for it on Amazon? Your review will help encourage others to read it.

I love writing guides like *The Time Chunking Method: A 10-Step Action Plan For Increasing Your Productivity*. I'm confident they'll help you squeeze more value out of each day. The problem is, without reviews, very few people will give this guide a chance.

Only a tiny percentage of readers leave reviews. Most folks don't. That's understandable since we're busier than ever these days. Having said that, I'd like to ask for your help in posting a quick review with your honest thoughts.

Here I am, knee bent and hat in hand, asking you to do that small favor for me. The more reviews I receive, the more people who will be willing to read this guide. That exposure will help me to create additional action guides and blueprints that make a real difference in others' lives.

Thanks in advance!

Author's Note

Writing this book has been a labor of joy and pain.

On the one hand, it's a fantastic feeling to finally finish it. A lot of folks are going to benefit from the material in this action guide. Knowing that it's going to improve their lives is gratifying beyond description.

On the other hand, *The Time Chunking Method: A 10-Step Action Plan For Increasing Your Productivity* took months to complete. That's a more time than I had anticipated. A lot more.

One of the reasons it took so long was that I wanted it to cover a mountain of material. That being the case, I spent a lot of time doing research before writing the book. Evernote was invaluable during this stage of the process.

Another reason it took so long is that I was completely ignorant abut how to actually publish it for the Kindle. It's one thing to write a book. It's another thing entirely to learn about formatting, covers, blurbs, book marketing, etc.

It has been a learning experience to say the least.

I know, I know… a lot of "experts" claim you can write a great Kindle book in a week if you just buy their special writing system. I have my doubts.

My next book will take less time. Having learned everything you can possible imagine about formatting, covers, blurbs and the rest will surely streamline my process. I'm already at work on it.

One last note before signing off…

I'm looking forward to hearing from you regarding how the time chunking method has improved your productivity. You can find me at ArtofProductivity.com. Be sure to sign up for my list to receive your free gift (I mentioned it at the beginning of this action guide). As a subscriber, you'll be among the first to find out about my future releases.

Damon Zahariades
http://www.ArtOfProductivity.com

Other Books by Damon Zahariades

Morning Makeover: How To Boost Your Productivity, Explode Your Energy, and Create An Extraordinary Life - One Morning At A Time!

Would you like to start each day on the right foot? Here's how to create quality morning routines that set you up for more daily success!

* * *

Fast Focus: A Quick-Start Guide To Mastering Your Attention, Ignoring Distractions, And Getting More Done In Less Time!

Are you constantly distracted? Does your mind wander after just a few minutes? Learn how to develop laser-sharp focus!

* * *

Small Habits Revolution: 10 Steps To Transforming Your Life Through The Power Of Mini Habits!

Got 5 minutes a day? Use this simple, effective plan for creating any new habit you desire!

* * *

To-Do List Formula: A Stress-Free Guide To Creating To-Do Lists That Work!

Finally! A step-by-step system for creating to-do lists that'll actually help you to get things done!

* * *

The 30-Day Productivity Plan: Break The 30 Bad Habits That Are Sabotaging Your Time Management - One Day At A Time!

Need a daily action plan to boost your productivity? This 30-day guide is the solution to your time management woes!

* * *

Digital Detox: Unplug To Reclaim Your Life

Addicted to technology? Here's how to disconnect and enjoy real, meaningful connections that lead to long-term happiness.

* * *

The Time Chunking Method: A 10-Step Action Plan For Increasing Your Productivity

It's one of the most popular time management strategies used today. Double your productivity with this easy 10-step system.

* * *

For a complete list, please visit
http://artofproductivity.com/my-books/

81181408R00095

Made in the USA
Middletown, DE
21 July 2018